MW00899702

If Bill Hale is a great storyteller—and he is ... er of the
open mind. These stories of memory and ... oth ... gated
world called Dunean, a small textile ... South Carolina during
the Great Depression and World War II. The vividness of these stories from
the author's life shows us no event or object is without meaning and charm: an
unplanned visit from the preacher, the top drawer of his dad's dresser, a can of
kerosene on the back porch, a mysterious Irishman passing through. The pull
of nostalgia is strong and sweet throughout, but it serves the higher purpose of
showing the creative power of a life deeply lived. If Bill Hale is a good man—
and he is—he is also a trickster who knows that charm works both ways. And
some of the stories are just funny as hell.

—Daniel Patterson, professor of English,
Central Michigan University

Bill Hale breaks into print at the tender age of eighty-seven, with beguiling
and evocative stories of his boyhood in the up-country of South Carolina three
quarters of a century ago. Devoid of political correctness or even a hint of
pretense, he draws us into the dusty mill village, unto his front porch, and into
his world—of apartheid, penny candy, itinerant "suitcase" weavers, and coffee
you eat. Laced with subtle humor and poignant and penetrating observations
about life and human behavior, Hale's book takes us on a slow, riveting waltz
through seven decades, teaching us the value of living in the present and of
listening, deeply, to life. A lifelong teacher, school principal, veteran public
speaker, and a fountain of profound wisdom, Hale entertains with astonishing
intellectual acuity. This is a book that leaves you thinking about your own story
long after you've finished reading his.

—John Bechtel, ghostwriter and literary consultant

When I read Bill Hale's manuscript, I smiled, laughed, empathized, and shed
a few tears with his stories. One doesn't have to be a Southerner raised in
a mill village in South Carolina to identify with the universal themes and
lessons he covers in this touching memoir. These poignant, disarmingly honest,
unforgettable stories remind me to stay in touch with my own.

—Trannie Abbouhi, retired teacher of creative writing,
South Carolina High School

THE VILLAGE

— *and* —

BEYOND

MEMOIRS OF A COTTON MILL BOY:
A COLLECTION OF STORIES ABOUT
PEOPLE, PLACE, AND PURPOSE

WILLIAM HALE

iUniverse LLC
Bloomington

THE VILLAGE AND BEYOND
MEMOIRS OF A COTTON MILL BOY

Copyright © 2014 William Hale.

All rights reserved. No part of this book may be used or reproduced by any means, graphic, electronic, or mechanical, including photocopying, recording, taping or by any information storage retrieval system without the written permission of the publisher except in the case of brief quotations embodied in critical articles and reviews.

iUniverse books may be ordered through booksellers or by contacting:

iUniverse
1663 Liberty Drive
Bloomington, IN 47403
www.iuniverse.com
1-800-Authors (1-800-288-4677)

Because of the dynamic nature of the Internet, any web addresses or links contained in this book may have changed since publication and may no longer be valid. The views expressed in this work are solely those of the author and do not necessarily reflect the views of the publisher, and the publisher hereby disclaims any responsibility for them.

Any people depicted in stock imagery provided by Thinkstock are models, and such images are being used for illustrative purposes only. Certain stock imagery © Thinkstock.

ISBN: 978-1-4917-2644-0 (sc)
ISBN: 978-1-4917-2647-1 (hc)
ISBN: 978-1-4917-2645-7 (e)

Library of Congress Control Number: 2014903347

Printed in the United States of America.

iUniverse rev. date: 03/31/2014

We all live in the same moments of time, but each person has his or her own filter through which to see the world. I dedicate these stories to my family, knowing full well they may see these times differently. No matter how the details may vary in our individual memories, we can all agree that we share a powerful love story. We lived in the Dunean Mill village of Greenville, South Carolina, during the Great Depression and the Second World War.

Contents

CHURCH

WORK

MISCELLANY

Preface

I ASKED MY PAPA, "WHERE did this village come from?" And in a voice of great wisdom and profundity, he said, "In the beginning, the people were naked because they had no clothes. They tried fig leaves and animal skins, but that was not comfortable. Then one day, from the heavenly sky, a big shower of seeds fell and covered the Southern land. Next came the rains, and the plants grew; some plants had huge white fluffy balls on them. The people learned how to make thread from that fluffy stuff—they called it cotton. Later, a man invented a loom to weave that cotton thread into cloth. The people loved cotton cloth and made their clothes from it. They built cotton mills. The workers had to have places to live, and that is where this village came from!"

Of course, that is not the way it happened. After the Civil War, the Southern states found themselves in a dilemma. They had a growing population of Scottish, Irish, Dutch, and German folk with talents passed on, generation to generation, from the crafts guilds that had preceded the industrial revolution. It was a large potential workforce without an industry. Meanwhile, each year millions of bales of cotton were being shipped to New England and Europe from the rich plantations throughout the South. Many saw this as an opportunity to create a new manufacturing system utilizing these immigrants' unique skills. So, in the years from 1880 to 1920, more than four thousand cotton factories were built along the eastern slope of the Appalachian Mountains, from Virginia to Alabama.

The labor in these mills was hard and the hours long. Before child labor and mandatory schooling laws were passed, nearly all family members would work in the mill. Large families were prized by the mill owners. Children of the workers were expected to join their parents in the factory when they were old enough, and they were often taken out of school at the age of seven or eight.

The factory villages were fairly self-contained, with cottages, a company store, churches, schools, and recreation facilities—all built to entice workers to the site. Power and water were supplied free, as was any maintenance. The houses were where future "hands" were produced to staff the mill; they were rented for a small fee taken from workers' pay envelopes.

My family, the Hales, were typical in the village. There was Papa (Bill), Mama (Mae), and in order of birth, George, Emma, Louise, Genieve, Edward, Billy (this author), Jessie Lou, Mary Anne, and Carol Ina. These family members, and my childhood friends and neighbors, are the characters in my book.

Our house was one of about two hundred in the village. It was located in the center of the village, within sight of the mill, the company store, churches, and the community gymnasium. US Highway 29, which runs from Maine to New Orleans, passed in front of our house. All of the houses in the village were constructed of clapboard and painted the same color, except for about ten houses on "Boss Boulevard." The bosses' houses were individually designed and most imposing.

I lived in the village eighteen years, during the Great Depression and World War II. The village still exists. The house where I grew up is there, but it now seems much too small to have been the stage for these stories.

I have written these stories in the hope that each reader will see his or her own story and begin to formulate them into some expression of art—whether that expression is in verse, song, painting, or more books. In *Listening to Your Life,* Frederick Beuchner said, "Write about what you really care about ... Write about what truly matters to you—not just things to catch the eye of the world but things of the world the way they have touched you to the quick, which is why you are writing about them. Write ... then the things that your book makes happen will be worth happening—things that make people who read them a little more alive, a little wiser, a little more beautiful ... in short, a little more human."

—William Hale

Acknowledgments

I WISH TO ACKNOWLEDGE SOME of the people who helped me develop these stories into a book: my wife, Helen, whose marvelous memory of times past and ability to tell stories gave wings to my memory; my children and grandchildren, whose cyber dexterity aided me greatly when I was faced with the computer and its antics; my friends who read an occasional story and told me, "These need to be published"; and my longtime secretary, Nancy Chandler, who took my rough-hewn typing and made it look professional. And I thank the luck of my good gene pool, so my life was long enough that I could tell these stories with a bit of historical perspective.

FAMILY

Night's Quiet

IN THE SUMMER MONTHS, ALL the windows would be open to bring in the coolness of the night. The village was quiet except for the constant buzz of the mill and the occasional whirl of traffic passing. The lonesome cry of a cat, the warning bark of a dog, the slamming of a door someplace, or someone talking in bed in another room might punctuate the deep quiet. Before sleep came, the music of the village always intrigued me. At age eleven, my freewheeling mind catalogued every sound. The quiet was a strange, wonderful gift of the night, a gift I can still open in my memory today.

If the wind was blowing, the scrape of a tree limb against the house might add its coda. Sometimes a roll of distant thunder would break the silence, making me uneasy. Or maybe I would hear the unexplainable *crink* of the house settling on its foundation of brick pillars. The stillness could also be disturbed by the soft sounds of my own body as my internal organs went about their business.

Those moments just before sleep, with the house open to the serenade coming from the village, were a haunting delight for me when I was a boy. My world had not yet accumulated so many things to regret or responsibilities to replay as sleep tried to overtake my consciousness. There was a deep feeling of freedom while I waited for sleep to come. Perhaps there is significant truth in the words of the song from the Broadway musical *Big River*: "Only once in your life are you free." As I grew older, the noises of the day I had just lived were often too loud for sleep to roll in gently as an ebb tide.

The houses in the village were built close to each other because the planners wanted to pack as many as possible on the available land. They were so close we were often entertained or annoyed by the sounds from the houses next door.

Mr. Garner was a strange sort of man who said very little, but his garden was the best on the block. He grew huge watermelons, with the vines entwined around his corn plants, and when they ripened, he shared them with the kids. On his back steps he would cut a melon in many slices and invite us to gather around and feast, but he never did much more than grunt and smile. Late at night after the "settling" had come, he would sit on his porch all alone and play his harmonica. He played mostly hymns, but occasionally he seemed to be composing something of his own. It was a soft sound, and you had to have "the ear" to hear it. Most people did not hear it, because their own sounds were too loud.

The night quiet was frequently disturbed subtly by a yell or shout in the distance. At other times it was disturbed in extraordinary ways. There were two families of Morgans, not related, who lived side by side on our block. They could not have been more different. The noises from their houses were polar opposites. One house emitted boisterous, chaotic, frightening sounds, while the other sent forth sad, scary, "sacred" noises. In both cases the sounds were some form of hollering or yelling.

One of the Morgan families had two teenage sons, Charlie and Louie, who were strong, athletic types—big strapping boys. Their daddy was a classic weekend drunk, and when he was drunk, he was mean, cantankerous, and violent—and he wanted to hurt somebody. For years, when they were younger, the boys just put up with his antics, but there came a time when they had grown up enough to take over. To protect their mother and themselves when he came home, the boys—who were fine Boy Scouts—started tying him with heavy ropes to a brick pillar under the house. He would be under there late into the night, cussing, raising hell, threatening everybody, and shouting. Then later, as the booze began to lose its grip, he would be pleading and promising to do right. Finally, they would untie him and let him in the house, and that part of the village would be quiet once more. Did tying him up like that cure him? No! It happened over and over again.

The other Morgan family had one teenage son. Unlike most of the village people, who attended the traditional Protestant churches provided by the mill, these Morgans were members of the Pentecostal Church of God, which was about a mile away. Their worship services were filled with shouting, speaking in the "unknown tongue," and being baptized with the Holy Spirit. They had a male quartet that sang jazzy, highly emotional songs, to which the congregation stood and moved about, clapping their hands to the beat. Mama called it "hiccup" singing because of the jerky cadence of the music. For a long time, this Morgan family would have a midweek prayer meeting at their house, which would begin after supper. As the village began to succumb to darkness, they would hit high gear, shouting, singing, and garbling the unknown tongue loud enough for gods to hear. It went on into the night. Lying in bed with those sounds whirling about made me feel weird and scared—the breakdown in common decorum gave me the creeps.

However, most nights were peaceful and serene, and sleep came easily to me, especially after a tough day of running everywhere, climbing trees, playing sandlot baseball, and letting my boyhood energy drive the minutes. When I was searching for sleep with the village at rest, it was like a sweet melody playing in the background. It had to be beneficial for my developing awareness of life to know that following the cacophony of daily activities there would be the symphony of sleep. This bred in me a fine-tuned security about the wonder of the cycle of each day.

Today we close all our windows and doors, so nothing from the outside can get to us, and we therefore live with artificial electric tones. We hear the constant hum of the air conditioner, the off-and-on cycle of the refrigerator, the dropping of ice that is endlessly being frozen, the flush of the toilet, the sound of rushing water in the sink, the crackling sound of the Woodwick candle that imitates a log burning in the fireplace, or the ping of the computer, signifying that a message has appeared there to be read.

I have to listen carefully these days to hear any sounds beyond our walls. Occasionally I can hear the splat of rain hitting the metal flashing around the chimney, the peal of our wind chimes, a car horn doing what it has to do, or the whining of the fire truck leaving the firehouse across the street. All these closed-up, contained sounds are comfortable and effective for a pleasant lifestyle, but they can never measure up to the peacefulness of the village slowing down and settling in for a night's rest and rejuvenation.

I can almost hear it now!

Calvin's Gift

I DON'T KNOW WHEN THAT big black Bible came into the family, but it was there from the beginning of my days. It had its own resting place on the bottom shelf of the mahogany table in the corner, near the settee in the front room. Never did I see anyone reading it. It was just there, like the rug or the lamp. My only excursions into that huge book were not to read the contents, which were scary and churchy. I occasionally would pick it up and lay it on the piano bench so I could read again names and dates that Mama or Papa had written years ago. Right smack in the middle of the huge, age-worn Bible were pages for recording family births and deaths, which dated back four generations. It thrilled me over and over to find my name, "Billy: July 25, 1926," listed with the births. That old book was a curiosity to me.

Summer days without school were times to explore the house or to plunder through dresser drawers that contained a wonder world of odd things—like an old half-torn picture of some old person, which has faded into more oldness; a broken pair of scissors, waiting for whatever you do to scissors that are broken; several bobbins of colorful sewing thread; and a discarded reed hook. Everything in that drawer generated curiosity.

However, around 1934 to 1935, my curiosity quotient was exceptionally low. There were no programs, people, or incentives to help me launch inquisitiveness in my life. I was seven or eight years old. I had never read a book for pleasure, nor did I own one until later in my life. Maybe all boys were that way—just not interested in probing *why* things were as they were.

One summer morning, an event occurred that changed my life. This particular morning, I was alone on the front-porch swing, which made two mesmerizing sounds as it went back and forth. One was the tinkle of the chains that looped over the two big hooks at the top; these chains were a few inches longer than necessary and struck each other as they swung forward and back. Along with this, there was a high-pitched squeak because the hooks had not been greased in a while.

It was rare for me to have the swing all to myself. Usually there would be two or three Hales swinging, but this morning it was mine alone. For variety, I turned over and rested on my belly. The swing came to a stop, and I focused on the cracks in the planks of the porch floor. A small line of ants caught my attention. Ants were moving back and forth, busily, and they were stopping to "kiss" each other as they passed. Why did ants never stop moving? The presence of ants normally called for a flit gun to kill them, but these ants were not bothering anybody. I do not recall how long I lay there on my belly looking at ants. It could have been a long time or just a fraction of a second, but I was temporarily relieved from the major issues in my life (mainly storms and church). A touch of curiosity had momentarily rescued me from the mundane and morbid and set me free to be just a boy.

My mind was usually locked into the present. I did not pursue ideas or things—I simply did not have the mental space to be aggressively curious. In school, books that were designed to propel young minds to probe had no effect on me. I never asked a "why" question in school as Billy Pruitt or Dot Gilmore, who were from educated families, did.

The young boy lying belly down in the swing needed a push, a shove, a launching pad; he needed something or someone to jump-start his curiosity. To paraphrase and combine separate quotes from writers Frederick Beuchner and Carlyle Marney, I counsel, "Never underestimate the power in any one moment of time, because therein may lie the fibers from which you can weave the fabric of life someday—including this moment. Listen to your life—it is happening right now! Listen—listen."

Too often, significant moments pass by unheeded and underutilized; they fade ever so quietly into the cracks of our own history. It is the cavalcade of lived moments that make up our history and become the words of the master narrative of who we are. The boy in the swing was about to have one of those moments. Would he listen and store it, or would he let it become part of life's detritus?

It happened often in the summertime. We would all be gathered in the kitchen for lunch, and there would be a rapping at the front door. Someone would go down that long hall and soon shout back, "Calvin's here." Mama would cringe. She knew from past experience that he would stay a few days. Calvin would be uninvited, and he'd show up like the wind on our porch. Calvin was the older son of Mama's brother, Peb, who lived about twenty miles away, in the small mill village of Lyman, South Carolina. One of five children, Calvin was fourteen or fifteen at this time, tall, lanky, and bony—an Ichabod Crane sort of guy. My brother who was about Calvin's age would have nothing to do with him, so I became the only family member who would hang out with him.

Mama would give Calvin a blanket and let him sleep behind the settee in the front room, as far away from us as possible because, as she said, "He don't smell right." Calvin was a hobo, a vagabond, rough and tumble. He stayed just this side of breaking the law. They could not keep him at home, school, church, or in the village. He would be gone for days without a word. Calvin was a total embarrassment to his family.

Our family would visit Calvin's family from time to time on a Sunday afternoon, if Papa could get someone in the village to drive us up there, because we had no family car. Mama would ask about their children, skipping over Calvin because she did not want to embarrass Aunt Eva.

Calvin and I spent most of the days together during his visit. He carried a rick-rack paddle in his back pocket. It did not have the rubber band with a ball attached; it was as empty as the plate on our dining room table on Sunday where the fried chicken had been. He used it to knock rocks or a handful of china berries, sending them into orbit. Calvin and I would sit perched near the top of the chinaberry tree in our backyard, from where we could see the neighborhood, watch folks hanging clothes on the line, or see cars and trucks pass by the front of our house. Calvin loved to talk. Sometimes we just sat "nesting in the gale." He would harvest chinaberries for later sending into orbit.

Calvin had been everywhere! Why, he had been all the way to Atlanta, Georgia. I knew I would never go that far! He would take his finger and snap it really hard against his paddle—*snap*—and say, "Billy, that's the way it sounds when a 'cracker' knocks a homer out of Ponce de Leon Park," and my mind would travel to a place I had never seen. He had been to the ocean, and he told me, "Billy, you can stand there, and it keeps coming at you and never gets there." Calvin had been to Birmingham, Alabama, and he told me it looked as if a thunderstorm was about to happen all the time because the smoke from the steel mills covered the sky.

Calvin had been to New Orleans several times. He had eaten shrimp, which I had never heard of, and that would set my mind off on another trip to a fascinating city. "If you go down Canal Street and turn right, it will take you to where the pretty girls are."

Every time he started talking about the girls, Mama would hear him—even if she was on the other side of the village. She would shout, "Billy, don't listen to him; he's crazy as a loon." Right in front of him she would say that.

Early each morning, I would run down the hall into the front room and jump up on the settee with both knees to see if he was still there. If he was, it would be "fantasy land" again that day. Inevitably, one morning he would be gone, just like the wind, his blanket folded in the most meticulous detail as if to say, "Thank you, Aunt Mae, for letting me stay a day or two."

I had perhaps two or three Calvin visits over the summers of my boyhood, cajoling me now from time to time to recall those beautiful hours in the top of the chinaberry tree. Then the visits stopped. I lost contact with him, but memories of Calvin stayed with me.

Over the years, families scatter, become absorbed in new venues, adventures, and relationships, and they forget aunts, uncles, cousins, and even grandparents. As the decades passed, I heard an occasional tidbit concerning Calvin's whereabouts, most of it just rumor: armed robbery, prisoner in an Alabama jail, escaped, recaptured. I heard once that he was in Hawaii. Then one day a telephone call came, and someone said, "Thought you might want to know that Calvin died." I never heard that an obituary or memorial service of any kind was carried out in his honor. It was simple—Calvin had died!

I could not let that stand. I decided to write my own eulogy to Calvin and mail it to his surviving family, but I never got around to it.

Calvin gave me the most precious gift of all, and it was not a trinket from his travels or his favorite rick-rack paddle. No, Calvin gave me the gift of *curiosity*. It was his tales of places and events that caused me to dive with passion into books at school. I wanted to find Atlanta, the oceans, Birmingham, New Orleans, and much more. In so doing, I discovered my great loves of geography and history, which became my keys to learning.

Yes, I should have written that eulogy and said these things to his family. Perhaps now the words that I have written can serve as some consolation for that lost opportunity.

Never underestimate the power in any one moment—even if it is simply "nesting in the gale" in the top of a chinaberry tree.

Never miss a Calvin just because "he don't smell good."

Azzie's Wash Stick

You cannot live the next chapter of life successfully
if you do not know the story so far.

BREAKFAST WAS SERVED TWO TIMES each morning when I was a boy. Those who had to be at work at six thirty ate about six o'clock, and the "schoolers" ate about eight o'clock. Breakfast was mostly biscuits crumbled in coffee, with a lot of sugar and milk. We ate our coffee. Mama would sit with us and have a second cup of coffee because she had eaten earlier with those who went to work.

What we talked about around the table is now forgotten, faded into the dark recesses of my mind—except for one or two things Mama said that later in my life resounded with wisdom. I learned to use the phrase, "Mama used to say ..." when I wanted to make her sound wiser.

It was also around the table that Mama gave us many injunctions that shaped who we became. Some were profound, and others had a bit of levity in them. More times than I can recall, she said, "Remember, you can have manners even if you ain't got no sense," and then she'd ruffle up my hair and laugh. Another one of Mama's profound statements was delivered in a heavier tone. She had experienced something that prompted it, but we did not know what. She would say, "Remember, you are better than nobody out there, and there is nobody better than you." Many years would pass by before I sensed what she really meant by that statement.

During the Depression years, my family had to watch our money very closely. The mill only operated a few days a week, and it was the sole source of income, except for the cashing in of insurance policies, which Mama had to resort to. She had to skip making other payments, at times, to make ends meet, but she always found enough to pay Azzie Logan to wash and iron our clothes each week. Azzie came on Mondays to wash and back on Tuesdays to iron. Mama paid her one dollar each week. Azzie lived about two miles from our village, in a section of Greenville where the black population was segregated from the whites. She was about Mama's age and had the same body build. Her husband had left, and she rarely heard from him. They had a boy, R. C., whom we got to know.

Even on the coldest or hottest days, she would walk to our house, arriving early. Before I got out of bed I would hear Mama and Azzie talking and laughing, about what I do not know. They had fun together in those early-morning encounters—two women with nothing separating them but their names. Azzie loved me, and I felt it. She would pull me into her abundant breast, holding me softly, messing up my hair, and saying, "You just like my R. C."

There was something comforting about waking up to the sound of Azzie chopping wood so she could build a fire under the big black three-legged wash pot. I could lie there and from the sounds tell what she was doing. After the chopping would come the clanging of the three huge washtubs, which all week hung on nails on the side of the house. Then I would hear the whine of the hose filling each with water. She did all this before coming in the back door to speak to Mama or any of us who were having breakfast.

The laundry stove—why it was called that I never knew—in the corner of the kitchen always had a kettle of water boiling, and it made a gurgling sound. Azzie would come in, go to the ice box, and see what was left over from supper the night before. She'd put it in a round biscuit pan and heat it on top of the stove. She stood behind the stove and ate on cold mornings, even if there was an empty chair at the table, but most of the time she took her breakfast and sat on the back steps. Sometimes it was only a few turnip greens or mashed potatoes. Sometimes it was just a few spoons of several foods. I knew that Mama always prepared a little extra to make sure there was some for Azzie the next day. Mama's relationship with Azzie went to a deeper place than either of them knew.

She had been our washwoman for many years, perhaps before I was born. Where or how she'd obtained her wash stick I do not know, but she had it all the time she came to our house. It was a "picker stick," which was used on the looms at the mill to knock the shuttle through the threads. It was about two and a half feet long and made of exceptionally hard wood, highly polished and finished with a yellow stain. She kept it in a certain place, stuck through the lattice near the washstand. The only other one I had seen was in the possession of a boy on the back side of the village. They used it as a ball bat when they played "side up," which was what we called it when two sides were chosen to play.

Only once did I dare to move her wash stick, and I put it back in the wrong place. The next time she came to wash clothes, she told Mama she had to hunt for her wash stick. Mama said, "I saw Billy playing with it the other day." Azzie never said anything to me about it, but Mama made it plain to me I was never, ever to touch her wash stick, because she'd brought it from her house a long time ago. "That stick's got a long story," she said. After that, I never saw her with it without wondering, *What story?*

Three number 3 washtubs hung on the back of the house. Azzie used one with soapy water and the rub board, another was filled with clear water for rinsing, and the other looked like the ocean, blue as the sky; it was for bleaching white clothes and sheets. Many wash days in the summer I begged her to leave the blue tub filled so I could play in it. With a Popsicle stick for a diving board and one of my sisters' dime-store glass dolls, I could have them diving in the ocean, far distant from my backyard. I'd continue this until my hands were blue and wrinkled.

Azzie had dreams, and she paid close attention to see whether there was a number in any of them. If there was, she would gamble that number with a bookie in her neighborhood. She called it playing "Pete." Occasionally she would win a dollar or two. She was a mysterious lady.

Mama and Azzie understood that when we were in the backyard on wash day, she was our mama. She was in charge of us, and we behaved as she told us to. She let us help her, especially when she hung the clothes on the line to dry. I loved to sit in the chinaberry tree, listening and watching the clothes flap in the wind.

On cold mornings, after walking two miles in the bitter cold, Azzie would come in and ask Mama for "two thumbs full of Vicks salve," which she used to push into her nostrils for it to do whatever it did. She also put one thumb full in her mouth and swallowed it with a taste of coffee. I guessed it was her medicine. Again, she was an exciting and unusual lady.

In the summer months, I would beg Azzie to bring her son, R. C., with her some days. He and I were about the same age. When he did come, we had "yard fun"; we knew not to go out of the yard, especially together. On those days when we had lunch, the family would sit around the table in the kitchen. Azzie and R. C. would be given a plate each and they would sit on the back steps. We ate together and even passed some conversation and laughs. We ate together, yet we were miles and cultures apart. When R. C. came, my village buddies did not come around. He and I made a fortress one day. A fresh load of wood had been delivered a few days before; it was to be chopped into firewood. The wood was five foot long, split logs, which we stacked into a three-storied fort. We played there all day.

"Don't y'all get hurt."

"Watch out for splinters, Billy."

"Y'all better tear that down, R. C., cause we going to be leaving in a while."

We never saw our differences, because we were "soldiers."

In January 1934, when Papa died, Azzie came and took over the kitchen and other things as she saw fit. I had mumps and could not go to the funeral. I stayed at home with Azzie and my little baby sister, Carol Ina. We sat on the front steps as the family got into those long black cars and pulled away. Azzie sang hymns, some of which I had never heard sung at our church. Every once in a while she would ruffle up my hair and hug me. She invented a game we could play using the cars going back and forth on the highway in front of our house. "Billy, you count the cars going up the hill, and Carol and me are going to count the ones going down the hill, and whoever gets to ten first wins." Later on the rest of the family came back, and we went into the house. A preacher was there, and he said a prayer. It was only later that I wondered where they had gone in those big black cars.

Once I asked Azzie, "Why are your hands white inside?" We were standing by the washstand, with those three huge tubs brimming with water.

She took my hand, put it in her hand, and said, "De Lord started to make me white like you, but He stopped," and throwing her head back, she laughed big and hearty, ruffled up my hair, and said, "You won't do, boy!"

We had fun most of the time when she came. Not often, but sometimes, it would be different. Azzie would show up but not with her usual big voice and broad smile. She would just matter-of-factly go about her way, not saying anything or maybe only a soft-spoken word or two to Mama. No fooling around. She would not even hum, as she usually did. She wouldn't sing any songs as she rubbed the clothes over the washboard. This always made me sad. It was like a storm brewing somewhere that was heading our way. I would stay away from the backyard on those days after Mama said, "Leave her alone today." When I asked what was wrong with Azzie, Mama would say, "That sorry man of hers is probably back bothering her."

I'd never thought of Azzie being in a family or living in a house. I'd never thought of her as having a bed or her own clothes to wash. All of a sudden, the mystical, mythical curious lady, Azzie, lost some of her fun. Before that bit of reality hit me, she had been like an actress who came on the stage in our backyard. She was a great, wonderful black woman who brought the sunshine with her to dry our clothes and a playful spirit to make me happy.

Azzie continued coming to wash and iron our clothes for a long time. When I got my new trumpet, so I could be in the school band, I showed it to Azzie one day and told her, "I don't know how to play it yet."

She took it in her hands and rubbed it, pressing the keys down and looking in the bell. It was as if she were blessing it. "Why, Billy Boy, you'll be playing this thing just like Mr. Louis before you know it."

There came a time when Azzie stopped coming. Because of the war, and marriage, the family began to disperse, and Mama moved in with one of the older children. We no longer needed Azzie at our house. Mama passed her on the street a few times in uptown Greenville, and she always asked about us. The black wash pot was left turned upside down. The tubs hung silently on their nails on the outside wall, and her wash stick stayed stuck in the lattice near the washstand until it disappeared. I still wonder: *What was its story?*

I never learned to play the trumpet very well, but I did find out who "Mr. Louis" was. He was Satchmo, Mr. Louis Armstrong. Occasionally, when I hear a recording of Mr. Louis playing "Hello, Dolly," I remember Azzie and what a fun place our backyard was on Mondays back in those summer days of my boyhood.

It is tragic that we don't recognize how someone is making life better for us until the time is long past. I never had the opportunity to tell Azzie how much she made a little boy's life sparkle at times. And yet I can still feel her black hand in mine, feel her ruffling my hair, and hear her say, "You want me to leave the blue water?"

"Go Brush the Green off Your Teeth"

WHEN I WAS BORN, LOUISE was eleven, so I was her baby brother. It stayed like that for the rest of our lives. She was the family clown, the cutup, the play-it-by-ear piano player, church choir member, and my big sister. Hands down she was Papa's favorite—and Mama's difficulty. Louise was beautiful, vivacious, witty, clever, and she really, really liked me. Despite the gap in our ages, we were buddies. Our lives together did not last long enough; she was gone before I was a teenager, and my life was never the same. At night, when we were all in bed, she would sing to us, softly and soothingly, "A preacher went out hunting on a cold and frosty morn," or "Now, honey, you stay in your own backyard; don't mind what them white folks do."

Louise had quit school to go work in the mill at the age of fourteen, and when she was in her late teens, she had several suitors in the village. One was Clifford Wallace, son of the vice president of the mill. They lived in the second-most-imposing house of the village, on Smythe Avenue, where all the bosses lived. Clifford was a crippled man, with one leg shorter than the other. People said he had been born that way. He wore one shoe with a very high heel, but he still walked with a limp. For Christmas he made Louise a scale model of a three-masted schooner. It was the most fascinating thing I had ever seen. It was mostly black but had colorful flags. For years it was the centerpiece on our living room "fireboard," which was our family word for fireplace mantel. I cannot count the number of times I stood looking at that ship sailing the deep, blue sea, riding the waves that I had never seen. I could hardly believe someone had actually made that sailing ship with his own hands. Clifford was a good man.

Another man she dated was the son of our village policeman, Paul Compton. Paul was also a crippled man, after a wreck he and his brother had been in, in which they'd both nearly been killed. Paul had a pronounced limp. He gave Louise a pound box of Whitman's Sampler, and she shared it generously with all of us. Paul was the choir director at our church, and he asked Louise to sing many solos and to sing duets with him. Paul was a good man too.

This was during the aftermath of the Great Depression, before the mills returned to full-time operation. Many young men who worked in the textile world moved around the South, trying to find steady work. Several came to our village, and among them was a man who pursued Louise and was a friend of my older brother. Charles McBride was a "suitcase weaver" traveling around the Carolinas. He would try to find a set of looms to run for a while, and then he would go on to some other place. Louise dated him a few times in our parlor, which was across the hall from where the family sat. When they came in, Mama would say, "Y'all keep that door open."

A couple of times Charles called me over to the room they were sitting in and told me he would give me a nickel if I would go make them an onion sandwich, which was sliced onion and mustard on loaf bread. Sometimes, just to make a nickel, I would go to the door and say, "Y'all want an onion sandwich?" I liked him! Then, one night, he had laid his overcoat on the bed across the hall from where they dated, and I saw the top of a pint liquor bottle sticking out of the pocket. Because our minister constantly railed and ranted about the evils of "the devil in the bottle," that really scared me. I did not want Louise to ever see him again. I never spoke to him after that. I decided Charles McBride was a very bad man.

For years I wished I had told her I'd seen the liquor bottle and that I did not think she should be with a man who drank liquor. Later I would come to realize that she knew he had liquor and had probably drunk some herself. Yeah, Charles McBride was a bad man.

Then along came Gordon Walker, another suitcase weaver, seeking a job at our mill. Louise and Gordon met at the drugstore one day, and he was smitten immediately with her charm and good looks. They dated that weekend, and about two weeks later he came back to see her. Mama really did like this man. Gordon Walker was handsome, a Virginian, a sweet man, and he bragged about Mama's pound cake and fried chicken. Louise and Gordon exchanged letters for a week or two, and then one Friday he showed up at our house and said to Mama, "Mae." He had called her Mae from the start. "Mae, I've come to take Louise back to Virginia with me," and he did. A quickly arranged wedding took place at the altar of the church on Sunday afternoon, with Mama and my oldest sister there to witness it. Then Louise was off, gone out of my world, and that left a big hole in my heart. But Gordon Walker was a fine man.

Louise loved to sit down at the piano in the hall and sing at the top of her lungs, "If I had the wings of an angel, over these prison walls I would fly." You could hear her all over the house, and it made us all happy to hear it. Louise sat in the front row of the choir on Sunday, and when the preacher got too heavy on some topic, would look at me and wink, taking the sting out of the situation.

Louise stayed out much too late on dates, worrying Mama so much that she walked the floor, and when Louise did come home, they went into the kitchen, closed the door, and fussed real loud. I could hear them. One such night, when they were fussing, Mama said accusingly, "You been drinking, ain't you? I can smell it." This caused a sick feeling in my stomach.

Louise would often say to me, "Billy, you want to dance?" This happened mostly on Saturday mornings, when she did not have to work. We would crank up the old Victrola, put on a record, and dance in the front room, even though the preacher said it was the road to hell. She was a beautiful girl, taller than me by a foot, with a sparkle in her smile, and she held me close. I was conscious of her softness and was as happy as I could be. One day when we were dancing, she shoved me back from her and said, "I ain't gonna dance with you until you go brush the green off your teeth." I went immediately to get the toothbrush, dipped it in the baking soda box, and brushed real hard. Then I went back and we danced some more.

We did not have toothbrushes or toothpaste at our house. There was one toothbrush lying on the ledge at the kitchen sink for anyone who intended to brush his or her teeth. When every nickel had to be used to buy food, some things were simply not important.

After Louise went to Virginia, she wrote Mama every week, and I searched those letters for any message just for me. Only once did I find one: "Tell Billy I said to be a good boy and help you bring in the coal." There was a line in one of the first letters she wrote that made me happy, "Mama, I am learning to love this man more and more each day."

As I grew up and time passed, my contact with Louise was infrequent, but what I did hear about her distressed me: "Louise is drinking too much." She became an alcoholic and created for Gordon and their children a home that was filled with rancor and total unpredictability. She was an embarrassment to Gordon, who had risen to the executive level in the mill in Wallace, North Carolina. He needed a wife to be of help in their social life. Louise died relatively early, as a hopeless alcoholic whose legacy was chaos and disturbance in her home.

At her funeral I sat there, my mind jumping with my memories. I remembered that pint of liquor in Charles McBride's coat pocket, and I hated him. Did he start it? Maybe if I had said something to her it could have helped. In my youthful innocence, I believed it would have served as a deterrent because we were the best of buddies. Later in life I became fully aware of the fact that alcoholism is a disease, but I still believe that perhaps a word spoken would have helped.

It is chilling to my spirit to recall the several telephone calls I received, after I became the principal of a high school, from a drunken, besotted, weeping Louise. She called to tell me how much she missed Papa, who had been dead more than twenty years. Thick-tongued, she asked, "Do you still love me, Billy?" I tried to assure her that I did, but she did not listen.

I prefer to remember those weekends when she and Gordon would surprise us with a visit for a few days. They would park their car a block away from our house, and she would sneak around houses and get into our house without anyone seeing her, sit down at the piano and, with real gusto, sing, "She'll be coming around the mountain when she comes!"

Then there would be a blast of, "Louise is here! Louise is here!" Her voice thrilled me and made my heart jump. She brightened up the whole weekend. Gordon always gave the children a quarter, which was a big coin, enough to last a week.

Several years ago, Helen and I decided to take ballroom dancing lessons at the nearby YWCO because we were having opportunities to dance as we traveled more. After dinner on Thursday evenings we went for lessons. The last thing I did before we left the house to go dancing was to brush my teeth with great vigor. I considered it just good common manners and hygiene—or did I hear an echo from my days with Louise, when she'd said, "Go brush the green off your teeth"?

Depression Fudge

THE LONG DECADE OF THE 1930s, the time of the worldwide Depression, was a time when fortunes fell and desperate men leapt from skyscrapers to their deaths rather than face the throes of poverty. My family came of age during in this time. There was no "grinding and gnashing of teeth" around my house. No one panicked or cried, "Woe is me!" Everybody seemed to be at home or working. When all your neighbors are in the same plight, what you do is survive and help your neighbor survive.

Papa's attitude toward the times is evident in this comment made to Mama. It could be apocryphal, even though it was characteristic of his indefatigable spirit. "Mae, we might have to stand in the breadline, but heck, we might meet some new people there."

He had no savings account, no checkbook, nor money hidden away someplace. There was a small amount of money from cashing in several insurance policies, but that lasted only a week or two. It was not the end of the world, just the end of the rope. People held on, believing things would get better.

The mills closed, but people stayed rent-free in the houses, which belonged to the company. Electricity and water were given as part of the rent, so those necessities were available. If the mill did not close totally, the word *curtail* became operative. "Curtail" meant the work week was reduced to maybe one day a week. People had time on their hands, time for unusual activities.

Lard, the most vicious compound ever devised to clog arteries, was the staple frying component in our house. It came in three-pound cans with handles, and we called them lard buckets. Lard looked like very thick white paint and was used in all biscuits and cornbread; it was even added to dried beans and vegetables. Mama never threw away a lard bucket. She used them to water plants and for various other purposes.

One morning in July 1933, Papa suggested we go blackberry picking over in the railroad cut on the west side of the village. It was exciting to do something with Papa; it was rare that he was not at work. Papa, Mama, Louise, Edward, Genieve, and I, each holding a lard bucket, headed across the village to the railroad cut, which was lined with vines of all kinds, including big, succulent blackberries. This was the source of the train noise we heard late in the night, horns sounding a low, cautious moaning as they approached each crossing. This was the same railroad cut that was constantly forbidden: "Don't ever go play in the cut—that red dirt will never come out of your overalls, and you might get killed." It was there we would go and sacrifice a copper penny by laying it on the track, so the train would flatten it into a long, funny-shaped penny as a pocket souvenir. We also would lay two straight pins, crossed, on the track, to make a pair of "scissors."

We picked blackberries that day, eating our fill as we worked. We found a plum tree loaded with nice yellow fruit. While we were there, we heard a train whistle blowing in the distance. We hurried to the top of the cut to stand as the train passed by, waving at the engineer and receiving a wave back, plus a small toot of the whistle. Our blackberries made two huge cobblers over the next few days. Cobblers taste better when you go over to the railroad cut and pick them yourself.

Papa was restless. He was a village leader, and with the help and enthusiasm of Louise, he organized an amateur show to take place in the Masonic Lodge Hall, which was located above the company store. Several people from the village performed in the show. There was a boy who tap-danced while his mother played the piano; my sister Louise sat at the piano and sang "O Danny Boy"; two men played a guitar duet; the barbershop quartet—which actually had two barbers from the village barbershop—sang a funny tune about a man and a horse, which made everybody laugh, and "she" played the piano. "She" was a blonde teenager with a fine figure, pretty as a movie star. "She" sat down at the piano and played Rachmaninoff's "Prelude in C Sharp Minor." It was real music! One of the Garren boys sang—no one knew he had such a beautiful voice. The winner was to receive a ten-pound sack of flour from the company store. "She" won, and I was glad. For months I hummed the familiar part of the prelude and remembered the lovely girl at the piano. Thinking of her started a something new in my life, a dim light flickering that called me toward the future. Was it the prelude or her? *Prelude to what?*

This might have been the Depression, but for me it was *impressive* to have so many folks at home and doing fun things.

Papa, with the help of Mr. Green, an official at the mill, organized a baseball league made up of players from each of the mill villages around Greenville. It would eventually become the highly regarded King Cotton League. On Saturday afternoons, the ballpark became a general gathering place for most everybody on the village. Oh, there were a few spoilsports in the village, notably those "holy rollers" who went to the Church of God, where they spoke in unknown tongues and shouted in their services. We had to pass by a couple of these families on the way to the ballpark. They stood on their front porches and heckled us, "Y'all going to hell if you go to them ball games."

Mama would tell us, "Look straight ahead—don't even look at them; they ain't right!" There they were again! Why did some church folk rail so loudly about people having a good time?

It cost a nickel to get into the game, unless you wanted to stand outside and try for the foul balls that came over the grandstand. That got you in free, and then you had a nickel for a bag of peanuts. I was lucky—that happened to me several times.

Sometime early in their marriage, Papa had been in town one day and seen a big platter in the window of one of the department stores, big enough to hold a huge turkey. Being gifted with the talent of surprise, he bought it as a gift for Mama. It was too big to fit in any one of the cabinets, so Mama kept it in the top of one of the clothes closets. I had never seen it used until one day Papa took it into the kitchen and washed it. Then he proceeded to mix up the ingredients to make chocolate fudge. I had never seen Papa cooking! In a big bowl he put cocoa, sugar, and a stick of butter and stirred it rapidly. Then he put that in a boiler with some milk. He was humming all the time he cooked. I stood right beside the table, watching. It began to bubble. "Here's the secret, Billy," he told me. He filled a glass full of water and, with the spoon, took a drop of chocolate and let it fall into the water. "If it makes a little ball, it's ready." He tried a couple of times and then, like magic, it made a little ball of chocolate in the bottom of the glass. "She's ready, Billy!" He took some more butter, spread it all over the big platter, and poured in the chocolate, filling it to the edge. "Gotta let it cool," he said then.

About that time, Mama walked in. "I'll clean up your mess, Bill," she said.

"Mae, me and Billy made some real good fudge." I did not know I had helped!

Later, we all enjoyed his fudge. If this was the Depression, it did not seem bad to me.

Only a few times do I remember seeing Papa and Mama talking softly and seriously about things. They were sitting on the back steps one morning, side by side. Papa was smoking a roll-your-own cigarette, and Mama had a dishrag in her hand. Papa squeezed her on the knee and said, "Mae, we gonna make it. Mr. Roosevelt is going to get us back to work real soon—you just watch."

Mama said in a whisper, "Emmer brought me a five-dollar bill this morning—her and Will are so good to us."

"Mae, we will pay them back someday, you wait and see."

"I'll stretch it out just as far as it will go."

My sister Emmer and her husband, Will, had only one child and had saved a little bit of money. They lived about a block away. She was the oldest of the nine children, and she shared what they had. This is one of the ways families survived in these toughest of financial times.

Papa finished his cigarette and flipped the butt out into the dirt of the backyard. Mama got up and went toward the pear tree to see whether one was ripe. When she got up, Papa pinched her on the butt and said, "Mae, you know you are pretty—don't cha?"

This reminds me of a recent song, which said, "He's got a way about him"—my Papa did!

The Devil's Hole

WHERE AZZIE DUMPED THE WASH water after washing our clothes, the grass grew with great profusion, and the ground stayed moist all the time. It was the perfect place to dig for big, healthy earthworms for fishing. More than a few times, I took the hoe and an empty tin can and dug for worms. They were always there waiting for me to come and take them away. I would dig a dozen or more and put some dirt back on top of them to make them happy for their next adventure. These diggings were prompted by Will Vickery. Often he would say, "Dig a few, and we will go fishing after I come home from work."

In every family there is at least one character who is different in myriad ways; this person occupies his or her own mind space and essence. No one knows what another person is thinking in his or her true center of privacy. Some people, I believe, think in a language that is not expressible with the tongue. There are people who smile because from their inner world they have just entertained an amusing idea. Will Vickery smiled a lot, and he was different—wise, witty, and a wonderful source of curiosity for me.

When Papa died, Will's best friend died. They were great conversationalists when they sat down to enjoy a smoke. They liked their beers and an occasional snort of stronger stuff, privately. Talking about baseball was at the top of their agendas, plus politics, community and mill issues, and words. They both were intrigued with words and liked to inform each other when they had found a new one in the newspaper. "Billy, your Papa was one of the smartest men in the town," Will often told me. And my chest always swelled with pride.

As a boy, I never had an air rifle. Many of the guys in the village owned them. I never aimed my slingshot at a bird or anything alive. I did not like to roam in the woods adjacent to our village, as my buddies did. The woods actually made me uneasy. I was not a "nature boy," preferring the streets or the gym and my own backyard as my play space.

Will Vickery was a fisherman, and his tackle box was filled with wonderful little things. He had a couple of rods and reels, and he often brought home enough fish for supper. He fished alone, primarily because he was a quiet man and fishing allowed him to get away from the noise of family and just be Will.

I never knew it for certain, but I believe that at one of Will's many bedside chats with Papa when he was dying from stomach cancer, Papa said, "Will, take care of my little Billy for me." From day one of our grief, Will involved me in his fishing. He had never involved me before, except to dig his bait for a nickel.

Some days Will would send word by one of my sisters, who worked in the mill with him, "Tell Billy to dig us some worms, and we will go to the dam and fish." I would dig in the moist spot in the yard and get us a dozen or two worms to "feed the fish for their supper"—this is what Will often said with a laugh. When we got to the dam, Will would fix me up with a pole and show me how to bait the hook. Then he would go about twenty yards away and begin casting. I used the worms. He used artificial lures, which sparkled like Christmas ornaments. We did not talk much nor did we catch any fish, but I really enjoyed being there, just the two of us. On the way home, we would stop to get a "cocola" and share a pack of peanuts. Over the fishing season, we went to the dam several times. These were not great memorable moments when they happened, just good, peaceful times, but as the big clock passed on, they turned to gold.

I did have one unforgettable fishing trip with him, though. He had an older sister, Lilly, who lived in a big two-story farmhouse up in the country near Pickens, South Carolina. She was married to Warner Cox, a big-framed man with a loud voice. He and Will had fished many times, and they liked each other. They also liked their snorts of "white lightning."

One day about midweek, Will was passing by while I was up in the chinaberry tree. I yelled to him, and he waved as he headed toward the tree. I met him under the tree. "Billy," he said, "do you want to go fishing this weekend? Me and Emmer are going up to Pickens to visit my sister, and Warren wants to take me to the Devil's Hole to fish."

I checked with Mama, and then I asked him, "Will, why do they call it the Devil's Hole?"

With a smile on his face, he said, "Because that's where the devil lives!"—and he winked at me.

The next afternoon, a Friday, we drove to the house where the Cox family lived. It was very run down and had not been painted in years. The barn out back was leaning, about to fall. This was in the middle of the Great Depression, and they didn't have money for upkeep. The whole place looked shabby, but inside it was cozy and warm and the aroma of cooking apples swelled my anticipation of something good. After a big farm supper, which ended with some apple cobbler, we loaded into Warner's truck, three men up front—Warner's son came along. I rode in the flatbed as we drove out into near darkness. I found out we would need to park and walk to the Devil's Hole. As we walked, it got darker and darker. "Will, are we about there?" I asked. He assured me we were getting close. We crawled through a barbed-wire fence, my shirt caught on the wire, and I thought, *I wish Mama had told them I couldn't go.* My shirt tore a little. As we walked around a deep gorge, it got even darker, and the clouds started weeping a little. I had never been so uncomfortable nor scared in all my life. I'd heard someone say the plan was to fish all night. I did not cry—eleven-year-old boys don't cry—but I felt like it.

After what seemed a year, we finally began to hear the rush of the river. "This is Devil's Hole," Warner said. How had he found it in the pitch dark? It stopped raining, and they built a fire. Will helped me bait my line and found me a place to stand. He went about ten feet away and dropped a line; it was too dark for casting. I whispered to Will, "Are we gonna stay all night?"

"I don't know; Warner really likes being up here."

"I really do hope we go back tonight," I said in a pleading voice.

I tried to pull my line out of the water but couldn't. "My line is stuck on something, Will." He came over and jerked the line, and a big fish came up with it.

"Look what you caught!" It was a three-pound catfish. The excitement did not relieve me of wanting to go back to the house. The Devil's Hole was really living up to its name, as far as I was concerned!

It started to rain again. Warner came over to talk to Will about something, and Will showed him the fish I'd caught. "That's a good Stewart," he said.

It was a three-pound Stewart catfish. I had never heard of one before. I had caught a very unusual fish. They talked a little more, and they each took a snort from a fruit jar, and the rain came down harder. "Let's go! We are not fishing here tonight," Warner said with an air of finality. I could have hugged his neck. The walk back was not as long as the walk there. I had my big Stewart on a string; it flopped against my leg as we walked in the dark and rain.

At home, Lilly let us in. She wore a long nightgown. "Too wet to fish tonight. Billy caught the only one, but it's a Stewart," Warner said. He handed my fish to Lilly, who took it to the kitchen. Because my clothes were soaking wet, I slept in the nude, upstairs with their son in a feather bed, which wrapped around me like the safe, soft wings of a mother hen. I woke up to the smell of ham frying. Lilly served us a breakfast fit for a bunch of fishermen who had been out all night.

I spent the morning playing in the hay in the loft of the barn and tossing rocks at the crows who were eating the corn tossed out for the yard chickens. Before we left for home, we sat down for a big bowl of steamy catfish stew with big chunks of fish and corn. We were eating my Stewart. I did not say anything about it, because suddenly it dawned on me: they were saying "stewer"—not Stewart—because the fish was big enough to make a family fish stew!

I had been to the Devil's Hole and planned to never do that again. If there really was a devil, I was convinced that's where he would live. One trip there made me want to get to heaven.

Surprise

H E COULD TELL YOU THE batting average of each member of the New York Yankees baseball team. He loved to discover new words. He could add up a long column of numbers in his head, accurately. I never saw him do it, but he could leap over big buildings, stop a freight train, and fly through the sky. He was ebullient, politically astute, aggressively friendly to everybody, and generous even when he was broke. He made sure that Mae, his wife, had everything she needed and wanted and was happy. He was the type of man who would take our last quarter, go to the company store, and buy a big sack of sweet crackers. He'd come home and we would have a cookie festival on the front porch. He loved surprises, especially those he could pull off himself. (That apple does not fall far from the tree.) We called him Papa.

Bending over my bed one day, way before sunrise and before he headed out to work, he whispered in my ear, "Be ready after I get home from work 'cause we are going uptown. We got something to do."

It was a cold, rainy day when I got up to go to school, and I hoped the weather would not cause Papa to call off our trip uptown. All day long in school my mind jumped over the hours until the time for our mysterious trip: "We got something to do."

We lived two blocks from the streetcar station. The old streetcar amazed me. It swayed from side to side and made clanking, cracking, and screeching sounds as it swirled through the red-clay banks of the streetcar line. The seats were of brown hard leather. The conductor wore a round black cap that had ventilation holes on the sides. He was very friendly but also businesslike, with a coin change holder on his belt. The streetcar never turned around. It came to the end of the line, as it did in our village, where the conductor opened a little window and pulled a rope to disengage the wheel that rode along an electric wire and hooked the pole over a hook. He closed the window, picked up his lunch pail, walked to the other end—moving seat backs as he went so they would face the front—opened a window, and engaged a wheel to the electric wire. The streetcar was ready to go to the other end of the line. I loved to watch this conversion process.

When I came home from school, Mama helped me take a bath, in a number 3 washtub behind the stove in the kitchen, and she combed my hair. Papa kissed everybody, saying again, "Me and Billy got something to do uptown."

We walked hand in hand down the street. As we passed the boardinghouse, some man yelled, "Bill, y'all going someplace?"

Papa said again, "Yeah! Me and Billy got something to do uptown."

We passed children playing in their yards, and I felt sorry for them because I was getting to do something they were not.

At the streetcar station, we sat down to wait, and soon we heard it coming. It passed us and went about two hundred yards, where the conductor made that exciting conversion, and then he headed back our way. As we got on, Papa said to him, "How you doing today, Charlie?" Papa knew everybody and everybody knew him.

"Y'all going uptown?"

"Yeah! Me and Billy got something to do." Papa smiled and winked at me.

The trolley squeaked and swayed on toward town. Papa said, "Do you know that boy named James Wood?"

"He's in Miss Pryon's room with me," I said.

Papa then told me that since James' papa had died the Woods were having a tough time, and he thought it would be good if we bought James some clothes. "Don't you think that would be a nice thing to do? He's about your same size. How's about that?"

I said, "That is good." I was more impressed about going uptown with Papa than with what we were going to do.

He got off first and lifted me down from the high steps of the streetcar; we were in the middle of Main Street. The biggest store in town was J. C. Penney, and we walked right in. Papa spoke and nodded to everybody as if he were running for office. We passed through the store, heading to the boys' department, where I first tried on a pair of black boots with high tops and hooks to lace them up. Next thing was a pair of brown riding pants, whose legs went down inside the boots. "Bet he will like that," Papa said. While I tried on the outfit, Papa and the salesman talked about folks they both knew. "How about a leather jacket?" Papa said. When I put it on, I felt warm, and I secretly wished it were for me. It had a thousand silver buttons and was lined with real sheep's wool. The outfit was complete, except for the final piece: an aviator cap with a pair of goggles. It was black, just like the jacket. Again I felt just a touch of envy for James Wood because the jacket and cap made me feel strong and big.

"Now, let's put it all on and see how it looks." We went in a little room and put it all on, placing my old clothes in a stack on a bench. When I came out, we went to the mirrors to see the transformation. I looked great. Papa and the man talked about it, and I stood there admiring how I looked. "You like that, Billy?" Papa asked.

"I sure do."

"Well, it's yours."

We never talked about the switch from James Wood to me. That was what my Papa lived for: *a big surprise!*

I kept the new clothes on, carrying my other clothes in a J. C. Penney sack as we walked up Main Street toward the Carolina Theater. Papa spoke to everybody, tipping his fedora, especially to the women, and stopping to shake hands and chat for a minute with some men. Every store we passed, I looked in the windows to see a reflection of me in my new outfit. I probably strutted a little bit.

At the theater, the lady at the ticket office asked, "Bill, where's Mae?"

"She couldn't come today, just me and Billy."

The lady looked me over and said, "You all dressed up today."

"It's all new," I said proudly.

In the theater, Papa never sat down but stood at the back wall overlooking the seats. He sat me up on the wall. We watched *Little Women* on the screen.

Before we got on the streetcar, Papa went to the drugstore and bought a bag of chocolate soldiers for us to eat on the ride home.

Could a boy ever have had a better day or a Papa more enjoying doing what he liked to do best of all? Surprise!

"Helen Hendrix, Look at the Stars"

I OVERHEARD MAMA, GEORGE, AND Louise talking about "the trip" one morning while they ate their breakfast. "But it's gonna cost nine dollars," Mama said. George and Louise told her they could come up with the money, and she ought to tell Mr. Simmons she wanted to go; it would be a once-in-a-lifetime thing to do. The trip was organized by Mr. Simmons, who ran one of the village boardinghouses and owned a huge truck.

The world premiere of the movie made from the great classic *Gone with the Wind* was taking place in Atlanta at the Loew's Grand Theater; the year was 1939. Mr. Simmons planned a one-day trip for as many as a dozen village women to go see the movie. The movie had broken all decency codes by allowing Clark Gable to use the word *damn* on the screen. He had promised the women a side trip to tour the Fabulous Fox Theater with its ceiling of sparkling stars.

On a Saturday morning, about fifteen women met in front of the company store to load for the trip. Mama, in Sunday dress complete with a hat, pocketbook, and lunch sack, climbed up the little ladder at the back of the truck to take her seat under the canvas that covered the truck. I was scared. Mama had never done anything like that before. "I'll be back directly," she said as the motor started and they pulled away. The truck left the village about eight o'clock in the morning and was to return at nine that night. The nine-dollar cost for the trip was for a ticket to see the movie and to pay for gas. I thought all day about Mama being gone so far away.

We were all standing there waiting when the truck came in sight. It was about to turn dark, and I wanted Mama to be at home before it got dark. When the truck pulled up to the curb, I saw Mama get off, coming down the ladder backward. As we walked home, Louise asked, "Mama, did he really cuss in the movie?"

"He shore did—he said 'damn,'" she said, and she giggled a bit.

When we returned to the house, she sat at the kitchen table eating the supper we had saved for her and told us about the trip. She reached into her pocketbook and pulled out a postcard from the Fox Theater. "We looked up, and the whole ceiling was covered with stars, and they twinkled; it really looked like nighttime."

She seemed to be more excited with the Fox Theater than the movie she had seen. That picture postcard of the marquee of the fabulous Fox stayed in the top drawer of our secretary for years. Occasionally I would see it and try to imagine how they had made all those stars twinkle at the Fox. *That was seventy-five years ago, and those stars still twinkle!*

Seven years later—after high school and two years in the US Army, where I served as the drum major of the Seventh Division Band, mostly in Korea—I married Helen Hendrix, my first and only ever sweetheart. She was a drum majorette from our high-school band, and we got to see the sparkling stars at the Fox Theater with our own eyes.

On a Saturday afternoon filled with sunshine and promise, November 9, 1946, we boarded a train in Greenville, which was bound for Atlanta, for our honeymoon. By sheer coincidence, we were there during the world premiere of Disney's *Song of the South*. This was one of the first color movies to mix animation and live action together on the screen, and it brought to life forever the song "Zip-a-Dee-Doo-Dah." The premiere was at the Fox Theater. Our room was at the Winecoff Hotel, on the fifth floor, facing Peachtree Street, and we watched from our window the premiere's parade with all the characters from the movie riding in convertibles, including Barbara Hale, Bobby Driscoll, and Hattie McDaniel. It was an unexpected thrill.

One evening, we walked several blocks to the Fox Theater to see the movie. We arrived in time for a sing-along with the Mighty Mo organ. When we first arrived, we walked down front and looked up at the stars—they were awesome. The movie was truly memorable, but the stars were more so!

We checked out of the Winecoff Hotel on Friday, November 15, 1946. We were stunned, as the world was stunned, to hear that on the evening of December 7, 1946, just three weeks after we left, the hotel burned, killing 119 people, mostly 4-H Club members attending a weekend conference. It remains the most deadly hotel fire in the nation's history. In later years, with a bit of gallows humor, we claimed to have left smoldering embers there when we checked out. We never forgot the Fox Theater and those twinkling stars—they still sparkle!

Over the years of our wandering, before settling in Athens, Georgia, my wife and I became devotees of Broadway musicals but had to be content with the movie versions. We did not live close enough to the big centers where touring shows played, nor did we have sufficient disposable income to travel to see the Broadway shows on stage. Athens was near enough for us to see an occasional Broadway musical at the Fox Theater; it was the closest place for big touring shows. However, going just occasionally did not bode well for securing good seats. We bought tickets for the whole family several times—*A Chorus Line*, *The King and I*, and *Hello, Dolly*—but they were not very good seats. It was a special thrill to introduce the Fox and its fabulous starry ceiling to the grandchildren, and to be back at the place we'd enjoyed on our honeymoon.

By the 1980s, the Fox Theater had become the premiere venue for touring Broadway musicals in the South. We started going more frequently, on Sunday nights, still buying the best available seats to the big blockbusters like *South Pacific* and *Oklahoma*. The Fox Theater became the one place in all the world where we could be transported into myriad worlds by the best songs, the best voices, and the best seats. There is nothing quite as awesome as that moment when the lights dim, and you hear the first note of the overture, and you know that soon the huge curtain will open and invite you to a world totally removed from the present one and into the imaginative realms of musical theater.

We retired in 1988 and decided to become patron ticket holders at the Fox Theater, so we joined both series, "The Theater of the Stars," which was the summer shows, and "Broadway in Atlanta," which was the winter/spring shows. We got wonderful seats in the front orchestra. There were ten or twelve shows a year. We never felt richer than when we had, in our lockbox, our tickets for the next season in "our" seats. Making the switch from Sunday-night shows to the Saturday matinee allowed us time to have lunch on the way to the theater. It was a ritual, an extraordinary time of delight and anticipation.

Since 1988, we have traveled to the Fox Theater 190 times. For every Broadway show on tour, we have been in "our" seats, looking up at those stars and having flashbacks of history. For all our spending on international and domestic travel, the fine theme parks of Disney, and ballgames of varied sorts, we have never gotten more for our money than at the Fox. That old theater has been our family's "signature" for decades—oh, yeah! That smile on our faces, right now, is because our tickets for next season just came in the mail yesterday! Next year the stars will be twinkling, just as they did for Mama, way back in 1939.

Then I Knew

I ALWAYS WANTED TO PLEASE Mama! From time to time she would have sharp words with one of the adult children, and I would see the hurt in her eyes, and she would lose her jolliness. I never wanted to cause her eyes to go dim and watery. When I first began to sense her as a person, not just Mama, her many manifestations were hidden in the crevices, nooks, and wrinkles of moments lived. She was many different mamas and played many parts in my boyhood drama.

I remember when I was just barely tall enough to see over the kitchen table where she was making dough in her big wooden boat-shaped dough trough. She formed a big ball of dough and proceeded to pound her fist into it over and over. "Billy, you have to knead it real good to make them taste like biscuits." With her well-used rolling pin, she made a huge flat oval of dough and then took her biscuit cutter and, quick as a wink, filled two black baking pans with what looked like a hundred little round things ready to bake. She brushed off the extra flour from their tops with a hand towel and put them in the oven. *She was a baker!*

Many times, early in the morning, I sat with Mama in the coolness and shade of the front porch and watched her string the beans for lunch. She had a pot wedged between her knees and an apron full of green beans, stringing and snapping them into bite-size pieces. I helped her with some. "Make sure you get the strings off real good." *She was a cook!*

At the foot of her bed was Mama's "art gallery and creation room," topped most of the time with a white lacy scarf. When she opened her

Singer sewing machine and sat down, she was a Picasso or an Oscar de la Renta. Mama was a fine seamstress, and she became totally absorbed in the creative piece at hand. Frequently she hummed songs, which gave her delight as she fed colorful fabric under that needle, moving faster than your eye could see it move. At the same time, her feet danced on the pedal, which drove the whole process. She was a complete artist in the flow. *She was a seamstress!*

Sitting around the fireplace in a semicircle, especially in the winter months, we listened to the Philco radio. We loved the Tuesday night shows best: *The Jack Benny Program*, *The Fred Allen Show*, and *Fibber McGee and Molly*. While we listened, we all ate peanuts, but Mama had to eat them by pressing them against her bottom teeth with her finger because she had no upper teeth and did not wear the false ones after supper. She and Papa had false teeth, and they kept them during the night in two cups on the fireboard. The cups were filled with water so the teeth could soak all night. Their faces looked funny when they went to bed; with their teeth in the cups, their faces were broken at the mouth; they had collapsed faces. *She was the centerpiece of our family!*

I sat beside Mama in church. She mumbled the hymns softly and showed no emotion, neither delight nor disgust. She stared stone-faced at the preacher, who went about whatever preachers went about doing up there in the pulpit. Her hat was always cocked to one side, and the feather remained motionless during the whole service. What was she thinking? There were nine children to think about. Was she precooking dinner in her mind? Her mama was living across town with her baby sister—was her mind there? After the preaching was finally done and we had sung the hymn, she stood up, smiling, and became quite animated as she chatted with neighbors about whatever was the topic of concern. *She was a churchgoer!*

Usually there were four women from our block at the kitchen table when the Chinese checkers board was in action. Mama excelled at the game and could play two sides at the same time. The women always had a fun time. Loud laughter rang out of the kitchen into the yard, and we knew someone had told a tale. She taught me to play, cautioning me, "But don't ever take these marbles out to play pig's eye—I don't want them to get dirty." *She was a Chinese checkers player!*

Her garden was as good as any in the village, and she spent many hours pulling weeds, hoeing around the vegetables, and watering them with a lard bucket. I sat many evenings in my perch high in the chinaberry tree looking down at that lone woman tending to potential food for our table. I wondered what she was thinking. Occasionally she would stand, leaning on the hoe, and look around at all the houses as if she were wondering what those who lived in them were doing. *She was a gardener!*

Preparing three meals a day for a big family consumed the major part of her time. Often she was preparing for the next meal as she cleaned up from the last one. However, Mama would find a little speck of time just for herself, and when she did, we would hear her playing the old, out-of-tune piano in the hallway. She sang as she played, "Trust and obey, for there's no other way to be happy in Jesus but to trust and obey." Earlier in her life she had played the piano at the Piedmont Baptist Church, but she would not play it if anyone was around. We never disturbed her while she was in another world for a few minutes at the piano. What was she thinking? Was she remembering her two younger brothers who'd died before they had a chance to live very long? Truman had died at twelve of consumption, and Grady had died at seventeen. Perhaps she was visiting happier times when she was a carefree teenager without the responsibility of a family the size of a baseball team. *She was a stealthy musician!*

Mama never hesitated to remind me, sometimes as a rebuke and sometimes with tender regard, that I reminded her of her Bill, who was forty-nine when he died at the lowest point of the Depression. "You keep putting that much pepper on your potatoes and you'll die just like your Papa," she'd say. Or it might be, "Your hair with that big cowlick is just like your Papa's when we were courting." *She was a mother being a mother!*

Mama sometimes lost her calm demeanor and normal brightness. I could readily tell when her mood was sour. Her big smile and chuckle were gone and she would not "jive" with us. She walked faster, was impatient more, and was unresponsive to our antics. Louise would say, "Stay clear of Mama this morning—she's not happy today." At the breakfast table, she buried herself in the *Greenville News* and said nothing to us when we left for school. What was she thinking? Probably, how every day was the same, with no change in view: same old house, same old routines, without a sparkle. Did she feel trapped in a world she did not like? By the time we came in from school, Mama was back to her regular self. "Well, did you learn something at school today?" *She was a woman expressing a mood!*

When did this multifaceted woman become, in my eyes, more than the myriad assortment of mamas? At her brother's home in Lyman, South Carolina, one Sunday afternoon after lunch, she and Uncle "Peb" were talking about when they were children. I was sitting under the table, hiding from my sisters as they talked. "You know, Mae," Peb said, "he told a lie to get to go in the army. He was only sixteen, and seventeen when he was killed. Mae, he was just like my boy Calvin, so restless and always in trouble." He was talking about their young brother, Grady.

Mama said, "I remember the government man coming to our door and telling Mama and handing her a little bag of his things." Grady was buried in France in 1918. *She was a grieving sister!*

I left home to go into the army when I was eighteen. I had been drafted, and now Mama was at home with just her three young daughters. Her three sons were in the military forces, scattered overseas from Italy to Burma to Korea. A small blue banner with three red stars hung in the front-room window to indicate that we were in service. In the army, much time was spent chatting about things back home. Some guys told of activities they enjoyed with their dads, but most of the chat was about how great their mamas could cook. I heard of the "best-tasting Irish stew" ever made in Ohio, *pasta e fagioli* made in New York "fit for a king," and lamb chops with potato cakes served at the Mankey's house in Pittsburgh. I joined in telling them how wonderful Mama's pound cakes and yeast rolls tasted, how tough she was, how her garden was the best, and how she was a village champion at Chinese checkers. I bubbled on and on about my mama. I made her more than she was! I think all the guys did the same thing. I bragged about Mama and quoted her saying wise things she never said. We all made our mamas bigger than life and unique. In the telling, I created "Mama the person," a human being of great value and worth to me. It was then that I knew. *A legend without portfolio!*

Oh my God! What will my children tell about me someday in order to make me more than the sum of the parts?

The Kerosene Can

F OR YEARS I SAID, "WHEN I write my mama's story—and I shall do it—the title has to be 'Don't Get Sick.'" Well, she never actually said those words, but they were written deep in her psyche. This was a hard-core attitude played out on her stage. She meant it. It was not used as a suggestion; it was an edict. Mama was very dismissive about aches and pains. When did it start? Where did this part of her approach to life come from? I don't know, but this belief colored her view of the world: Be tough, be strong, and don't give in to illness when it comes your way.

Mama and I were sitting by the fire; she was ninety years old. My family and I were visiting her in the home of my youngest sister, Carol Ina Patterson, with whom she was living at the time. I asked Mama, "How far back can you remember something in your life?"

She hesitated for a long minute and said, "I remember our house, up near Tigerville, at a place called Blackbottom; it was a big white house with a chimney at each end. I was about two years old. Mama had wallpapered the house with newspaper to keep us warm. I remember seeing words on the walls and pictures of clothes."

I urged her on with, "How long did you live there?"

"We moved when I was about four, to live in Laurens, South Carolina."

"Then where did you move?"

"We moved to the mill village at Piedmont, but we lived there only two years and they made us move."

"Mama, nobody can make you move."

Quickly she said, "Well, I just know my Papa was real sick because he contracted malaria, and they made us move out into the country on a farm."

There it was! A marker in the mind of a very young girl, a dreadful idea, had been planted, which would mature into an approach to personal health that would affect her family for generations to come. She never allowed herself to get sick. She was stoic—that was Mama! Keep a stiff upper lip and don't be weak, for "This too shall pass."

Papa was the opposite. He was Epicurean. His motto might have been "Live life to the hilt; you are here only one time." What an amazing combination they were!

Early in the 1930s the Hale family moved from Orr Mill in Anderson, South Carolina, to the last village they would ever live in, at Dunean Mill. Moving about from one mill village to another was no big deal for the Hales who, according to my oldest sister, had moved twenty times before she married and left the family. This move was significant especially for Mama. Papa decided they would not bring the old wood-burning kitchen stove but instead buy one of those New Perfection oil stoves. "Mae, we are not taking that old thing with us—it's time to get a real stove." It was then that an amazing liquid entered our lives: kerosene.

For the next twenty years, up until Mama "broke up housekeeping" and went to live with her oldest son and his family, we used kerosene. A five-gallon can of kerosene was kept on the back porch. It had a potato stuck on the spout; we never did eat that potato. The new oil stove worked well. It had six wicks, which burned the kerosene in bright circles of heat. Mama made some great-tasting dishes from that stove, especially her pound cakes, for which she was known village-wide. Kerosene was also the basic medicine available to us.

When you stubbed your toe, which was a common occurrence because we went without shoes all summer, you placed your toes in a little bowl of kerosene; it stopped the bleeding and instantly started to cure your toe. It worked like magic! When we had a croupy cough, Mama took a spoonful of sugar, dropped five or six drops of kerosene into it, and "down the hatch" it went in one awful gulp. Suddenly, the coughs were gone. That stuff was magic! There were days when you came home from school scratching your head; you had lice. After supper and right before bedtime, Mama took a handful of kerosene, doused your hair with it, and put a four-cornered handkerchief on your head; then you slept in it all night. Next morning the lice were gone, but your hair smelled like kerosene. The smell of kerosene in class was a telltale sign that somebody had "got the cure last night." Kerosene did not kill the lice. It made the environment so bad they chose to leave! That liquid was magic! Bites from mosquitoes, spiders, or bedbugs were handled easily with a dab of kerosene.

Papa used Mama's back-porch medicine can for a totally different task. The only heat we had was from four small coal-burning fireplaces, one in each room, except for the kitchen, which had aromatic warmth from the cooking that took place there. In the winter months, Papa got up first and built fires in the three fireplaces. However, he liked to kid around by saying whimsically, "I really hate to see Mae get up first and build the fires—that's why I sleep with my face to the wall." The procedure he followed was to wad up the previous day's newspaper, put it in the grate, put coal on top of it, and douse it all with kerosene. Standing back, he tossed a lighted match and watched it blossom into a roaring fire. If, however, there were smoldering coals hiding in the gray ashes from yesterday's fire, the fireplace and chimney would fill with fumes and when the match was tossed—*BOOM!* The windows would rattle, and a mushroom cloud would shoot out the top of the chimney, loaded with soot enough to cover houses for blocks and wake everybody up. The signal had been given that another day had begun in the village! By the time he had lit three fires, Mama would be in the kitchen lighting the burners on the New Perfection stove to get the oven ready for biscuits. Kerosene had become vital for survival in our house.

In defiance of Mama's nonspoken mantra, "Don't get sick," we caught colds and had stopped-up noses. There were two remedies that worked like magic. In a top drawer of her chest of drawers, Mama kept a pair of scissors and scraps of cloth left from cutting out homemade dresses, and there was a small jar of real medicine, Vicks salve. Before bedtime she would say, "Go bring me the salve and a piece of cloth." She would rub my chest with a good smear of the salve, warm the piece of cloth by the fire and then apply it to my chest, and I would sleep with it all night. Breathing the aroma of that warm salve made for a new day in the morning.

If you had a stubborn stopped-up nose, she put a glob of Vicks salve in a tablespoon, held a lighted match under it until the salve was melted, and then you sat around the fire and sniffed the fumes. It unclogged your nose, and if you smelled those fumes long enough, it would make you smarter because "Everybody knows you cannot think straight with a stopped-up nose."

"Don't swallow them seeds, or they will have to take out your appendix," she would say. We knew that apple seeds, orange seeds, watermelon seeds, pencil erasers, or fingernails went straight to our appendixes. No one in my family ever had to have the operation. For many years I wondered whether birds, which lived off of seeds, ever had appendicitis.

When you grow up in a family where being sick is not tolerated, you assume that all families have the same idea. When I married, I found out quickly that it was not true. When we had been married just a few weeks, Helen rolled over in the bed and said, "I think my kidneys have flared up." I was sure we had kidneys, but why would they choose to flare up? I did not know what to do! Was she saying she was sick? People didn't get sick! What I did not know was that in her family all you had to do was to say, "I don't feel good," and the whole family would serve as a staff of nurses until you got over your malady. Helen and I had to make some adjustments through the years when these two disparate approaches came into conflict. I still carry deep in my psyche the instruction "Don't get sick," and that has made me look as if I didn't care—but I did.

Occasionally, a doctor from uptown would make a house call somewhere in the village, and the news would travel like a wild grass fire all over the village: "They had to call the doctor!" This meant they were beyond the reach of kerosene.

The drugstore in the village was where we bought penny candy and ice-cream cones. The shelves were lined with little bottles of medicine that would cure almost any ailment we knew of, but I believe each bottle had just a little drop or two of kerosene in it to make sure it cured you.

Did Mama's "Don't get sick" commandment work? I don't know, but I do know she lived to be ninety-two without being sick, except for a cold or two, and all nine of her children lived well into their 80s or 90s, except for Louise. I wonder whether kerosene would have cured her alcoholism?

Wringing Their Necks

MAMA INVENTED "WINNIE SOUP" BECAUSE it was an easy way to prepare a one-dish meal and required very little cooking skill. Even though the package said weiners, we always called them "winnies," and still do to this day. Mama was not a good cook, but she dazzled us with her pound cake and yeast rolls. She did not take the time to cook with consistency, but bless her heart, she stayed at it three meals every day, on a Depression-era budget. This meant making the most out of the least. The evening meal for most of the year was cornbread and milk. In the winter months it would often be yeast rolls and syrup. Those suppers were a massive production. She made finger rolls and had to let them rise twice, pushing the fragrance all over the house and out into the neighborhood. There were always three or four big flat bread pans filled with rolls placed around the kitchen; they had to rise to double their size before baking. We all waited patiently; they were best right out of the oven. I particularly loved yeast-bread nights, because I got my fill.

I never developed a taste for the evening supper of cornbread and milk. I always wished Mama would buy a few loaves of bread and a few slices of boiled ham. I could take my slice of ham and cut it into four squares about two inches in size. I would make four sandwiches using an abundance of Duke's Mayonnaise; it was a festival of a supper. I was always "starving to death," rarely getting all I wanted. "Mama, is it about ready?" I must have asked her hundreds of times during those days.

The special meal of the week was Sunday dinner, after we had been to morning Sunday school and preaching. This meal gave Mama a chance to show off. She loved to cook and eat fried chicken. I liked it best when Mama would not stay for preaching but go home and get dinner started so the wait would not be long. Coming in from a too-long sermon and too-long singing of "Just as I Am," I found the aroma more heavenly than what we had talked about at church! That fragrance, a mingling of frying chicken, baking biscuits, green beans, and a pot of gravy, pushed my hunger to crisis level.

The crusty fried chicken had begun its journey to our table the previous Tuesday. Tuesday was the day the chicken man came by selling fryers "on the foot," and Mama bought three, which cost a dollar. The chicken man opened his box and handed Mama three squirming fryers, which she carried by their legs. "You want to carry them, Billy?" she'd kid me with a big Mama smile. One time I had tried to carry them, and two got away from me. It took the whole family a long time to chase them down. There was an old worn-out number 3 washtub under the house, which we used to keep the chickens until they were ready to prepare for Sunday dinner. Mama turned the tub upside down and carefully placed the feisty fryers under it, placing a half brick under the edge to give them air. Then she placed a big stick of stove wood on top to make sure they did not turn it over and escape their inevitable fate. All during the week we tossed bread scraps under the tub to fatten them for the journey to the huge serving platter.

Execution time was Saturday morning. After breakfast, Mama started a fire under the big black wash pot so she would have hot water available. "Billy, go get the chickens for us." Why I was selected to be the executioner I never knew. I had learned the process by watching Mama do it. Reaching under the tub where the chickens had spent their week with us, I grabbed two legs, hoping they were both attached to the same chicken. Holding the head tightly in my hand, I whirled the chicken around and around until the head separated and the headless chicken flopped, flipped, jumped, and quivered, splattering blood all over the dirt of the backyard. This procedure was followed by two more episodes. "Mama," I then yelled into the kitchen, "the chickens are ready."

Dipping the chickens in the hot water made it easier to pluck them clean of feathers. When they were clean, Mama took a piece of newspaper rolled like a stick, lit it from the fire under the wash pot, and holding each chicken by its legs, singed the fine little hairs off. The scene then moved to the kitchen, where she cut them into frying pieces. It was a fascinating process to witness. Each one yielded thirteen pieces: one neck, one back, one pulley bone, two breasts, two thighs, two drumsticks, two wings, one liver, and one gizzard. The thirty-nine pieces were placed in the ice box until the next day.

Cleaning up the scene of the "wringing of necks" was my job also. With a brush broom, I swept the whole backyard, making sure no blood showed and leaving a pattern in the dirt as an artistic conclusion to the slaughter.

Mama used two platters to serve the thirty-nine culinary morsels at Sunday dinner, one for each end of the huge table. The white meat was reserved for the grownups, who had us younger ones convinced that the dark meat tasted better. One privilege granted the executioner was the right to choose one of his favorite pieces from the platter. I always reached for the gizzard, which seemed to bring no protest.

During Sunday dinner there was always talk about whose turn it was to wash the dishes; since it was a rather big task, it took two, or sometimes three, to do it. Mama never washed dishes after Sunday dinner, and neither did the executioner. "Billy, let's you and me go sit in the swing," she'd say. I learned then that if you are willing to do the dirty work you will be rewarded.

Sunday dinner was the one chance each week when we all could sit around the table for a meal at the same time. We sat there in our Sunday go-to-meeting clothes because we wore them all day. We were heading back to church that night. Never was there any food left over from Sunday dinner. We were the original clean-plate club—except when it came to Mama's pound cake. Everybody who was anybody in the village knew of her pound cakes. At church, boyfriends and girlfriends of my older siblings would ask, "Was there any cake left?" They would come to our house for cake and to sing around the piano. Our house was a village gathering place, thanks to Mama's pound cakes and a bevy of pretty Hale girls.

Time never stands still very long. The company store soon began to supply chickens already cleaned and ready to be cut up. My neck-wringing days gave way to a more modern way of life, and the fried offerings on Sundays were never the same after that. I had lost my identity as the executioner and had to take my turn at washing the dishes.

There was one other culinary treat that delighted me from Mama's do-what-you-can-with-what-you-got approach to feeding the family. It was the aforementioned winnie soup, which was served on Tuesdays. Why Tuesdays? I will never know, but it turned Tuesdays into a special day for years and years. For a boy who stayed on the edge of starving to come home at lunch from school and have a big bowl of winnie soup, which gave the whole house an aroma of delight and joy, there was nothing better. Mama would caution, "Don't eat too many winnies; save the others some." The "others" were those who would get off work at two thirty and then have their dinner. I sat around the table with them as they talked of the mill and bosses—hoping there would be a little winnie soup left and I could have what was in the pot. It was an easy meal to prepare. Mama would open three large cans of tomatoes, put them in a pot, cut up three pounds of winnies in about a hundred small rounds, cook it all slowly until the winnies were tender, add salt, pepper, and a tad of sugar, and serve with an abundance of saltines.

Until this day, when I get an urge to pamper myself and my taste buds, I make a winnie soup. I introduced my grandson, Bo Hale, and my great-grandson, Will Howard, to this amazing, magical dish of old, and they loved it. Thanks, Mama! God, I still love it!

"Billy, Go Make It Rain"

WHEN THEY WERE IN THEIR late teens, both my mama and my papa knew they had to be free of the restrictions of their homes in Piedmont, where they worked in the mill. They had dated a few times and really did like each other. Mama said, "It was not love at first sight, but he was so handsome!" Leaving to go to work in the Brandon Mill in Greenville was their way of getting to be together. She lived with relatives, the only way her parents would allow her to move, and he lived in the community boardinghouse, which was just for single men. Shortly after going to Brandon, they were married. Bill Hale and Mae Howard would create a big, wonderful family of "hands" for the mill, a significant family for the several mill villages where they lived throughout their lives. Mama never told her story outright, but if you listened carefully, she revealed it over time.

She was one woman, but nine mamas. Each of her children could write her story and each of them would be different because each of us experienced Mama through our own perspective and desire to make her "our" mama. If the facts in this story aren't all accurate—don't sweat it! Mama exists in the image each of us created and even the "facts" are skewed by our need to tell a story.

I cannot tell her life story, but I can tell stories about her life, and if I choose to embellish them, decorate them with my desire to make her more or less than she was, that's my way to make "her story" in a way "our story." If for some reason it does not measure up to others' images—so be it!

For fifty years I was a professional speaker, which means I got paid for the activity. If Mama said everything I quoted her as saying, she would have been a walking reference book of witticisms, quips, absurdities, puns, and bits of deep wisdom. When speaking to a group, I would often forget who had made a statement I wanted to use, and I would paraphrase it and give Mama the credit. I used this ploy in order to project a "homey" context. She never said, "Be somebody, because anybody can be a nobody," but they never knew. I had just made that statement up or subliminally absorbed it in passing.

Of her ninety-two years, I only spent nineteen years living in the house over which she prevailed. She was thirty-nine when I was born and fifty-seven when I went into the army. I believe she really did like me— not that I got special treatment—because I was a "pleaser." I was always trying to make her happy. There were times when she had to discipline me, usually with a hickory stick broken from a bush and administered with some force to my legs. Summertime whippings were worse because I wore short pants.

Mama and Papa had nine children, and when Papa died eight of us were still at home. She must have felt grief, but she never showed it. From the time of Papa's death at age forty-nine, she faced the circumstances of life and survived. No one in the far-flung clan ever would face such a devastating moment as she did. She was a middle-aged, Depression-captured widow with eight children and the mill operating only two days a week. Only through a charge account at the company store could she make ends meet. We had to eat. As each of us reached legal age to work in the mill, we did. School and education were left behind, and we "graduated" to the status of mill hand. In our family, Mama handled all the finances. Pay envelopes were given to her unopened, and she gave each of us an allowance, the amount based on our ages.

As I said, I was a pleaser, especially toward Mama. Many were the summer nights when the heat of day still penetrated the air of our bedrooms. It would be muggy and stiflingly uncomfortable; we would be sweating in bed. Things would get quiet, and Mama would say, "Billy, go make it rain for us."

That's all she had to say. I would get up in my nightgown and, with bare feet, go outside and remove two big washtubs from the side of the house. I would place them upside down under the eaves of the house near Mama's window. Then, I would get the water hose and squirt water up onto the roof, causing "rain" to fall down onto those tubs. I would stay outside, causing rain, for several minutes. After I came back to bed, the drip-drip-drip would continue with increasing intervals of silence between the drops of water. "You made it rain real good tonight," Mama would say. I would be proud. This cozy sound helped us to go to sleep.

As a young lady, Mama had played the piano at church. From time to time, when no one was around, she sat at the piano, played, and sang "Let Me Call You Sweetheart." Was this her way of expressing and experiencing grief that she never showed openly after Papa's death? Perhaps it was a way to experience grief privately. I never saw her shed a tear after he died, but she would sit in front of the fire and stare it into white ash. She had to be strong, and showing emotion was not the way to do it.

Mae Hale had just turned forty-seven years old when her man died. They would have been married twenty-five years in a few more months. "We were planning on having our silver wedding anniversary and asking people to bring only silver," she said laughingly.

She had played the role as Papa's supporting actor on their stage. He had taken the lead parts, and she had followed proudly because he had been a dynamo, a spokesman for the village, a force to be considered, a politician's friend, a motivator, and a passionate, affectionate man. Papa had kissed all of us on the lips and hugged us tightly, like a Papa bear. After his death, just two months before his fiftieth birthday, Mama had to step into his place, and she was not the same type of person. Mae Hale was not a hugger or kisser. She became more and more stoic. A hug from Mama was not warm and bosomy but instead was bony and quick.

Mama planned the weekends with the church in mind. She made sure we had clean clothes, clean bodies, and Sunday dinner mostly prepared. She was not a deeply religious person. I never heard her pray, nor did she read the Bible. Religious talk did not pepper our conversations. However, we did not miss church. And we did complain about the long-winded ranting of A. Howard Wilson! We never said a blessing before a meal except when company came. Sunday was a quiet day in the village, and we stayed in our Sunday clothes all day because we went back to church on Sunday night.

Her home was the meeting place for all of her children's friends. After church on Sunday night, the young people headed for our house. "Mrs. Hale, you got any pound cake left?" She usually did. Mama taught us the basic routine of tithing our allowances. "Mama, is fifteen cents still just a penny to the church?"

Mae Hale wanted nice things but never had the resources to get them; Papa also wanted her to have fine things. While he was uptown one day, he bought for her a mahogany upright secretary. It was placed in a prominent place in the living room. It had three glassed-in bookcases at the top, a drop-down writing desk, and several little drawers and cubbyholes to put mail in. That piece of furniture stood as an example of what they would have liked to have all over the house. Compared with the rest of the furnishings, it was like a big nugget of gold in a scuttle of coal. This is where she sat to write letters to her three sons who went off to war.

Among Mama's many injunctions to all of us were two that have stood the test of time and memory. The first is "You can have manners even if you ain't got no sense." She always said it with a smile, but nonetheless the message was plain: Act better than you look. The other injunction, the grand Mae Hale injunction, was "Don't get sick!" She could dismiss your feeling sick with, "Go on to school; you will cool off after a while." If you sidled up to her one day and mentioned having a pain, she would say dismissively, "It is only a fart in you sideways."

When Papa died, she did not hesitate to go to the school and say to the teachers (as one of those teachers related to me much later in my life), "I am going to need a lot of help raising my children, and I want you to help me." What a woman! The teachers came by after school and sat with her on the porch or in the kitchen, while they had a cup of Mama's Russian tea and a piece of pound cake. Some of those teachers really acted in loco parentis.

Mama lived to be ninety-two and never went to the hospital except when she fell in the nursing home and broke her hip at age ninety. If she had lived in these times, she would have been a social activist, a politically alert woman, and she would have been tough. She was born in poverty, married in poverty, and raised her children in poverty, but she was never "poor" herself. When the mill company decided to put in sidewalks in front of the bosses' houses, Mama appeared in the mill office saying she expected sidewalks in front of her house also. She could act this way because she provided many good "hands" for the mill.

She never had any money of her own to spend until she started receiving her Social Security checks. She sent her second one back, telling them she had plenty left over from the first one.

In her early fifties, Mama was still a very comely woman and perhaps a bit furtively flirtatious. There were two men, both good, political friends of Papa's, who intrigued her. One was Babe Riddle, who worked in the mill and ran for sheriff, unsuccessfully, a couple of times. He would never walk by our house and see Mama on the porch that he didn't stop and chat while she stood leaning against the porch banister. They would talk a long time. When we kidded her about it, she always blushed and made some statement like, "Not that old man." Babe's wife had died a few years earlier, and he was a very eligible man. Mama never dated any man, but I think she liked old Babe.

Her other contact was with former Congressman Heyward Mahon, who owned Greenville's premiere men's clothing store. Papa had been his campaign manager in two or three villages when he ran for Congress, and Papa had taught him the ins and outs of village politics. On many Saturday mornings Mama put on her hat, caught the trolley, and went to town. She pampered herself occasionally by sitting at the lunch counter at Woolworth's and eating a ham-salad club sandwich, which she really loved. While in town she would often go by Heyward Mahon's store to "just say hey" and renew acquaintance. The congressman was a widower. She did not mind telling us about going by to see him. One Christmas she bought my brothers nice jackets from his store, and I bet she got a good price. I think Mama was capable of a flirtation or two because she was a fine, well-liked woman and was good company.

She had lived the greater part of a century, and she had lived it well. Any person who could fall asleep by imagining artificial rain as real had worked things out pretty well. Did the *drip, drip, drip* on those turned-over washtubs take her back to some comfortable place in her childhood? Was that the music that she and her man had loved so much in their young lives? Or was it the evidence that the storm had passed? My heart can dance at times when I remember those nights that I was Mama's rainmaker.

Mae Hale never allowed herself to get sick, so on Valentine's Day 1980, at the age of ninety-two, in her inimitable style, she said to herself, "I think I will go." And she did.

The Crack of Dawn

EORGE McCALL WAS A HUGE man in many ways, and he
adored my Papa, Uncle Bill to him. His wife, Jessie, was a lady
in a real Southern sense: quiet, demure, well-dressed, smiling,
and teacher-like. George was boisterous, funny, and jovial; he was a
motorcyclist and the superintendent of the mill in Pelzer, South Carolina,
which was only nineteen miles from our village.

In the early years of the 1930s and the closing years of Papa's
life, George and Jessie came to visit us frequently. This was before
there were telephones in many homes and in the days when relatives
came to visit without making arrangements or giving prior notice.
Spontaneous visits were the standard, and the phrase "we had
company" was common. Upon the arrival of George and Jessie for a
visit, our house took on the air of a carnival; gaiety abounded. There
would be laughter, joke telling, and always a good yarn from George
about the family of his youth. I loved those stories best of all because
he had always been in trouble of some kind. Their visit usually lasted
a couple of hours, and then they were gone, and our house returned
to its normal routines.

George was the son of Papa's oldest sister, Bernice. She and Papa and
his twin sister, Mary, were born twelve years apart. Bernice had to serve
as surrogate mother because their mama, Caroline, had been a "sickly"
woman. The village at Piedmont was the "cradle" where this family was
rocked into being. Pelzer, the home of George and Jessie, was only a short
distance further south, on Highway 29.

For me there were not many sights more thrilling than when I was perched in the top of my chinaberry tree and saw their Model A Ford rolling up in front of our house. I'd scurry down, announcing, "George and Jessie are here!" I had a very special deep feeling down inside that was filled when they came to see us. George gave me a lot of attention, probably because I was Papa's namesake and maybe because he and Jessie had no children. Those two men really loved each other, and I got caught in the afterglow. He would tousle my hair and with one arm hug me to his giant frame. While they were there, I usually sat on the floor at his feet and fondled his hand because he had a thumb that had been split when he was young. It looked like a tiny butt. How it got that way I never knew.

Most of the conversation as I recall was, "Tell me how old so-and-so is doing these days" or "Have you heard from the people over in Piedmont lately?"

George always had a story or joke to tell, and demure Jessie would caution him, "George, remember there are children in the room." He and Papa would try to outdo each other telling yarns. They both loved baseball and followed the activities of the major leagues with focused attention. They spoke of Babe Ruth, Lou Gehrig, Pee Wee Reese, and Dizzy Dean as if they were old acquaintances. They practiced the art of conversation with aplomb, knowing that good conversation is the mortar that holds the routine bricks of life in place!

One of their visits has a special place in my memory. After he and Jessie had been there awhile, George said, "Uncle Bill, have y'all heard what a man down in Anderson has discovered?"

"What's that?"

"He has discovered a way to hear the crack of dawn." George continued telling us about the process. "You have to wake up before first light, hold onto the iron bedposts with both hands, get as still as a vase on the mantle, stay real quiet, and then—*ping*—a wee sound, like a small bell. He swears he has heard it several times!"

Papa, going along with the yarn, said, "Well, I'll be John Brown! I never heard of that before. Where did you say he lives?"

"He used to live in Anderson."

"Where does he live now?"

"He's in the crazy house in Columbia!"

Laughter filled the room.

I was seven years old and did not catch the whole joke, but the idea of hearing the crack of dawn intrigued me. The strong power of suggestion had me in its grip. All of our beds had metal frames, and for several mornings I woke up real early, held on tightly with both hands to the posts, and lay very still—nothing! After a few times, I thought I must not be doing it right.

When Papa died, George came alone to visit and chat with Mama. They sat in the corner of the front room talking quietly, not like the usual jolly times. He was helping her work through her grief. Before he left, he became the old George, kidding and joking and giving the little ones a nickel. I knew he gave Mama some money before he left because for the next few days she bought us special things, such as apples, oranges, and cookies.

Papa had died in January 1934, and when the first Christmas without him approached, George must have told Mama, "Mae, we want to be here to see the kids open their Santa Claus gifts." Mama told us a few days before Christmas that George and Jessie would be with us for the opening of gifts; we would wait until they got there to enter the "Christmas room." Vivid in my mental picture gallery is seeing George McCall walk in the door, jolly as the old elf himself, carrying the biggest sack of oranges I had ever seen over his shoulder, and in his hand was an equally big sack of apples. "Merry Christmas, Hales!" He was big enough to fill the void—and he did.

After Mama had served the adults her traditional breakfast of oysters and eggs, which Papa had dearly loved, George and Jessie left to go back home. We had more fruit than the company store, and Christmas lasted all week.

In every family tree there are some names that have stars beside them because they have contributed significantly to what the family represents. Beside the names of George and Jessie we need to put a couple of bright, glowing stars.

The Real "Sound of Music"

IN THE WORLD OF MUSIC the word *leitmotif* refers to a musical phrase used to identify a member of the cast of an opera each time that person comes on stage. With a bit of imagination and twisting, the word *leitmotif* can refer to the tone, style, cadence, and purpose of the musical background heard in all homes, from castle to hovel. All homes have a dominant theme, a musical score in the background that speaks powerfully of their lifestyle.

Some homes have a musical score that blares like a military band: orderly, purposeful, on schedule, and well dressed. There are homes that sound like rock and roll: frenetic, loud, nonmelodic, and cluttered. Other homes might sound like a fine symphony, a jazz combo, or a church choir.

Our family has songs that are part of our character. Most families have songs that are part of the life and breath of their hours and days. Currently, the song most often heard in our family is a blessing we sing before meals. When the bigger clan gets together for a meal, we all hold hands in a huge circle and sing:

> Thank you, Lord,
> Thank you, Lord,
> For our being together,
> For this time, for this place,
> For your love around us.
> Fill us, Lord, with your peace and joy;

Let it glow forever.
Bless us Lord,
Bless this food,
Bless our homes forever. Amen.

When I was a very young boy, I slept on a pallet on the floor next to the bed of my older sisters. Often at night, when the lights were lowered and the world took on a quietness that moved all over us, I would say to my sister Louise, "Sing me a song." She would sing my favorite one:

Now, honey, you stay in your own backyard;
Don't mind what them white folks do.
Just stay out and play as long as you please,
But, honey, stay in your own backyard.

I loved that song because it gave me comfort and a picture, an image, to take into my dreams.

My Papa had two songs he would sing for us when we sat around the table after supper, especially on Friday nights. These were "The Preacher and the Bear" and "The Bible Baseball Song." I never knew why Friday nights were so different from all the other nights in the week, but they were. Papa would be in an entertaining mood and would sing these for us. Thanks to the outstanding memory of my big brother Edward, here are the words:

The Preacher and the Bear
A preacher went out a-hunting, it was on a Sunday morn;
It was against his religion, but he took a gun along.
He shot himself some very fine quail
Also a little bunny hare,
And on his way to preach that day
He met this great big grizzly bear.
The bear marched out into the middle of the road;

He marched by the preacher, you see.

The preacher got so excited

He climbed up a persimmon tree.

The bear sat down upon the ground;

The preacher got out on a limb,

Cast his eyes to the Lord in the skies,

And these words were said unto him:

"Oh Lord, didn't you deliver Daniel from the lion's den?

Also brother Jonah from the belly of the whale?

Also the three Hebrew children from the fiery furnace,

As the Good Book do declare?

Now Lord, if you can't help me, for goodness' sake,

Please don't help that bear!"

Papa had a good tenor voice. He often sang with impromptu quartets at the barbershop when things were going slowly there. Mr. Cartee had several paperback quartet song books on a shelf behind his supplies, just in case singing was the thing to do. Papa, Babe Riddle, Frank Garren, and Charlie Coleman would sing, and it usually drew a crowd. I loved to be there watching my Papa sing, especially when he would wink at me and smile. Another song Papa sang often to entertain us was this one:

The Bible Baseball Song

Deacon Jones addressed his congregation

To the roofless in the rain;

"Now folks, this is an aggravation

To the Reverend Jackson Smith, that's plain,

But I propose, good sisters and brothers,

For some funds to shingle up these leaks

That a ballgame we should play on

This Emancipation day."

But Sister Jones in angry tones did speak:

"That ain't no game for good church folks to play."

But Deacon Jones says,
"But does not the Good Book say
That Eve stole first and Adam second,
Saint Peter umpired the game;
That Rebecca went to the field with the pitcher,
While Ruth in the field won fame;
Goliath was struck out by David,
There was a base hit on Abel by Cain,
The prodigal son made one home run,
While brother Noah gave out checks for rain?"

When my sister Louise was in a funny mood, or when the family was around the table acting silly, she would sing this bit of nonsense:

While the organ peeled the bananas,
Lard was rendered by the choir;
While the sexton rang the dishrag,
Someone set the church on fire.
"Holy smoke!" the preacher shouted,
And in the rush he lost his hair;
Now his head resembles Heaven,
For there is no parting there.

These "fun" songs tell me a great deal about the family I grew up in. My parents and older siblings kept the family tone at the gay level most of the time. It is not just silly romanticism to believe this. Oh, sure, there was the common strife and rancor in my family, as there is at times in all families, but we always went back to the lighter side of life, and we sang.

When our children were very young, we sang as we traveled about the country in our car. One of the songs we sang was "Side by Side," written by Harry Woods. This was during the time when the youth of America were asserting their independence from authority and protesting institutions in society that had become meaningless or nonresponsive to human rights. The hippie rebellion had its music, and we made two of its famous songs—"If I Had a Hammer," written by Lee Hays and Pete Seeger, and "This Land Is Your Land," written by Woody Guthrie—part of our lives. We sang these songs accompanied by two ukuleles played by our children, Karen and Billy.

If I Had a Hammer
Lee Hays and Pete Seeger

If I had a hammer, I'd hammer in the morning;
I'd hammer in the evening, all over this land:
I'd hammer out danger,
I'd hammer out warning,
I'd hammer out love between
My brothers and my sisters
All over this land.

If I had a bell, I'd ring it in the morning;
I'd ring it in the evening, all over this land:
I'd ring out danger,
I'd ring out warning,
I'd ring out love between
My brothers and my sisters
All over this land.

If I had a song, I'd sing it in the morning;
I'd sing it in the evening, all over this land:
I'd sing out danger,
I'd sing out warning,
I'd sing out love between
My brothers and my sisters
All over this land.

Well, I've got a hammer,
And I've got a bell,
And I've got a song to sing
All over this land:
It's the hammer of justice,
It's the bell of freedom,
It's a song about love between
My brothers and sisters
All over this land.

Another song we sang was about the joy and delight of this great country.

This Land Is Your Land
Woody Guthrie

This land is your land, this land is my land,
From California to the New York Island,
From the redwood forest to the Gulf Stream waters,
This land was made for you and me.

As I was walking a ribbon of highway
I saw above me that endless skyway
I saw below me the golden valley
This land was made for you and me.

This land is your land, this land is my land
From California to the New York Island
From the redwood forest to the Gulf Stream waters
This land was made for you and me.

However, the song that usually was the starter for our traveling concerts was one very true to our condition.

Side by Side
Harry Woods

Oh, we ain't got a barrel of money;
Maybe we're ragged and funny,
But we travel along,
Singing our song,
Side by side.

Don't know what's comin' tomorrow;
Maybe it's trouble and sorrow,
But we'll travel the road,
Sharin' our load,
Side by side

Through all kinds of weather,
What if the sky should fall?
Just so long as we're together
It doesn't matter at all.

When they've all had their quarrels and parted,
We'll be the same as we started,
Just traveling along,
Singing our song,
Side by side.

All of the houses in our village had their own musical scores, and if you listened carefully, you'd notice the music was a fairly accurate expression of family personality. The old adage, "There's no place like home," a line from the classic song "Home Sweet Home," is a poignant reminder that our desire to return home is basically to hear our own music again, to feel the comfort of the familiar, and to touch base with our original musical scores. There is nothing more saddening than a home where the musical score has been destroyed and replaced by a musical score that is alien to the home. This circumstance can occur when family configurations are altered by the vicissitudes of life. Family reunions are noble attempts to hear the music again.

When my Papa died, our family musical score vanished. In the next decade the family would scatter, and now that musical score can only be heard through the greatest gifts ever developed in the human being, namely, imagination and memory.

The Top Drawer

RECALLING DRAMATIC EVENTS FROM THE deep past takes only a modicum of mental energy and skill. The big episodes seem to be readily available in our minds. However, attempting to find images of the thousands of hours between those big moments takes much more cogitation and perseverance. I was one of nine children living with Papa and Mama in a small house with no bathing facilities, no central heat, no running hot water, and no private place to call your own. Hour after hour of doing life, doing whatever life was offering, just moving about time and place, must have been satisfying and productive. I think I spent great amounts of time observing people doing things rather than doing very much myself. Well, maybe observing is a good form of doing something.

Food was a dominating factor in our house. It took a special woman like Mama to stay in constant planning mode to purchase, prepare, cook, serve, clean up, and start over for three meals a day, every day. She once said in response to hearing about so many women having nervous breakdowns, "I'd have had one too, but every time I thought about having one it was time to cook again." She cooked without any of the current kitchen aids but managed to put on our table, with an abundance of talent, the most delectable dishes. Some of my favorite times when I was just a small boy were spent standing and watching her make biscuits. "You want to help me?"

"No, ma'am, I'm just watching."

Like a machine, she created biscuits from flour and buttermilk, each one the same size as all the others, placing them like round white soldiers standing at attention in the huge pan blackened from years of baking.

Mama's hair was long; it fell past her shoulders when she had it down to wash. It was streaked with gray for as long as I remember. I used to watch her wash her hair at the kitchen sink. In the winter days she'd sit beside the fireplace to dry it, or in the summer days she'd sit in the bright sun on the back steps. She combed those long tresses, and then she did the most fascinating thing. In one nonstop movement, she made a ball of all her hair on top of her head. She never minded when I just watched her doing things. These were not the kind of moments filled with memory making. They were not significant times, just sweet time-filling in between now and the next meal. Thousands and thousands of hours of time-filling moments grace our stages but fall into the dustbins of our history because of their sheer magnitude. But like mortar holding bricks in place, those moments help keep us a complete story. Those time-filling moments also furnish the punctuation marks in life, which give it meaning, just as they do in these paragraphs.

"Billy, run out to the company store and get me a can of lard—tell 'em to charge it." Walking to the store was "in-between time," but along the way I made sure to grab a leaf from every tree I passed and to not step on a line on any sidewalk. I also pulled a certain kind of weed that grew beside the sidewalk, which allowed the stalk to turn loose and me to taste the sweetness. A boy's life is a symphony of time-filling moments and antics, such as picking up a rock and tossing it for no reason except to do it, or spontaneously cutting a cartwheel because he can. Coming back home from the grocery store with a sack with the lard, I tossed the sack in the air and caught it, over and over, all along making sure I did not step on a line in the sidewalk, because that would bring me bad luck. Once I failed to catch the sack and it hit the sidewalk, denting the can of lard. When I got home, Mama said, "Take this can back—they know better than to send me a dented can."

"Mama, I dropped it."

"Dropped it?" Sighing, she said, "Oh! Well, I guess I'll have to use it. Don't ever do that again. Do you hear me?"

The times between are filled with small dramas, if we will simply listen.

When I was ten years old, I had a "forever hunger." The time between meals seemed to last nearly a year. I lived at starvation's edge. "Mama, is it about done?" I asked over and over.

"I'll call you!"

While waiting for lunch to be ready, I roamed the house, staying close enough to hear "Ready!" I'd find a drawer to ramble through to see what was there. Top drawers were the best for rambling, and the top drawer of our chest of drawers was the best place of all. Top drawers are convenient for tossing something you are not yet quite ready to discard or you want to stash away for the future.

Also in that top drawer there was a spool of sewing thread with just a little thread left on it. It was enough, however, to use as a tether for some unfortunate June bug. The sewing thread was light enough to tie one end of it to a rear leg of a June bug and walk around the house with the June bug buzzing and flying like an insect war plane. When the call came, "Y'all come on, it's time to eat," I would tie the thread to a bush and leave my "friend" buzzing while we ate. After the meal was over, I would go to get my June bug, most often to find a limp piece of thread with one June bug leg lying on the ground, still tied to the thread. The June bug was free but had made a great sacrifice.

That top drawer was the place where Papa's fountain pen resided. It was a beautiful dark-blue fountain pen, called that because it had to be filled with ink before you could write with it. You filled it by pulling a small lever out while holding the point of the pen in the ink bottle, then releasing the lever slowly to cause suction, pulling ink into the pen's ink reservoir. It was a most fascinating process. Papa used that pen to write letters to the editors of the *Greenville News and Piedmont*, touting the fine "boys," the Dunean Mill Dynamos, who would take the field for the baseball team in the upcoming season. After his death, the fountain pen became a treasured item.

"Mama, is dinner ready?"

"No! I'll call you."

She does not know I'm starving to death!

The grown men in the family smoked cigarettes. *Grown* meant you worked in the mill. During the Depression, store-bought cigarettes cost too much. In that top drawer there was a most marvelous machine. It was a clever device for rolling your own. It was made of bright-red tin, and with his light touch, Papa could roll one nearly as good as one from a pack of Lucky Strikes. I used to sit at the kitchen table and watch him roll a few to take to work the next day. Sometimes he would let me push the lever across the top. "Go easy and steady; don't stop once you start," he'd say. I took that device out and smelled it. The fragrance of sweet tobacco lingered on the machine. I wondered why Papa smiled when the preacher said smoking was a sin.

"Mama, is it ready yet?"

In that top drawer I always found some bits of stuff that needed to be tossed in the trash: old matchbook covers with all the matches used up, a broken penny pencil of no more use, and scraps of paper. I wadded them up and went to the back porch to put them in the garbage. That's when I noticed the girl next door was helping her mother hang clothes on the line. I sat down on the steps to observe. She was a teenager blessed with a fine figure. When she bent over to get a garment from the tub, her short dress hiked up, and I caught a brief glimpse of her underpants. They were white! When they finished and were walking back to the house, she looked at me and waved and smiled. The future had winked at me.

"Mama, I'm starving!"

"It's about ready."

I went back to the top drawer to wait a while longer. In the very back of the drawer I found four or five hairpins—those small black, shiny things the girls put in their hair at night. My sisters seemed to wrangle over those things every night. "Somebody got all the hairpins!" I hated to hear them fuss. They kept them in a little dish on the fireboard. The pins had tough little spring devices, which they opened with their front teeth before using them to hold some rolled-up hair. I took the hairpins I had found and placed them in the dish on the fireboard. *Maybe they won't fuss tonight*, I thought.

"Y'all come on—dinner's ready!"

My life had been spared! I closed the top drawer that was loaded with a world of stories and imagination-enhancing items such as a stringless yo-yo, a roll of adhesive tape, two chewing-gum wrappers, and an old church bulletin saved because it had these words written inside, "Trumpet solo by Billy Hale: The Holy City."

Those in-between times are a major part of life that should be relished, savored, and revisited in order to touch the real flow of life. Waiting between meals was as much a part of life as Mama's pot of pinto beans and cornbread, but I did not know it then.

"Don't Ever Say That Outside of This House!"

THE PRIVATE LANGUAGE IN A family, the real chatter that resides there, gives a fairly good indication of the level of wit and the tone prevailing within the walls. All families have coined words, contractions, and nonsensical phrases that are understood by all who live there but would be utterly farcical to a visitor. Also, almost every family has a few well-selected cuss words that decorate their chatter. There is a tremendous difference between "cuss" words and "curse" words. Cussing is usually free of malice and destructive intent. It is like adding color to a black-and-white painting or having a free fall through language. Cursing, on the other hand, is fraught with emotion and disgust and has the qualities of violence and rancor at its core.

For those of us who were young, neither cussing nor cursing was permitted. We did have a few words or phrases we could use that mimicked cussing. When I got real mad, I could say "foot fire" to relieve me of my frustration, and I could also say "shoot" or "I'll be John Brown!" For years I was confused about cussing and the commandment not to take the Lord's name in vain. Since I did not know what those words meant, I translated them to mean any kind of cussing or cursing. I didn't say hell, darn, or durn, which were too close to saying damn. Cussing was a big sin, right up there next to smoking, gambling, and going to movies.

One ritual in our family related to cussing as a rite of passage on the day you went to work in the mill. On that day you were permitted to say "shit ass." After all, how else could you describe your boss to the family?

Every family has a bevy of words to express the bodily functions. We could say *poot* but not *fart*. *Dookey* and *hockey* were used, but not the universal word *shit*. We could *pee* but not *piss*. Any word faintly related to human sexuality was totally taboo. Apparently in all families, however, there are clever, cutesy coinages of words vaguely related to body parts, which sometimes are carried throughout life. Among such words were these: *bunky*, *tootle*, and *thang*. Our family life was filled with idiomatic terms other than cussing. Sometimes we used a completely nonsensical word to express a feeling or emotion. The word *hissy* in my family was used when anger or disgust was being expressed loudly, as in "she's throwing a hissy fit."

Some words did not make any sense at all. They are not in any dictionary that I ever saw. *Thingamajig, doololly, cobstob, hickey*—words like these bounced off our tongues with ease, and everybody knew what they meant. There were phrases that made no sense but we all understood, such as these: When a storm "came up" we quickly "raised the windows down." Why did we "cut out the lights"? Our three meals each day were breakfast, dinner, and supper. Lunch was placed in a sack and taken to work at the mill. We did not say goodnight but night-night.

One of the worst things you could call another member of the family was "a one-lunged Ethiopian" and the biggest number in the whole world was seventy-eleven or perhaps a blue billion.

If you could have listened in on our family patter in recent years you might have heard this mysterious phrase: "Gimme a Sam." Back before the ubiquitous cell phone or iPod, long-distance telephone calls were expensive. I traveled extensively, making speeches around the United States, and I stayed in contact with Helen everywhere I went. I would arrive in Chicago, Denver, or Memphis and want to let her to know I was safe on the ground. I would call home using a scheme we had devised earlier. I would place a person-to-person call to Sam Hutchins, a cousin of ours who lived in Walhalla, South Carolina. Helen would answer the telephone and hear, "This is a person-to-person call for Sam Hutchins."

"He's not here right now," she would reply, relieved to know I was at my destination and we had not incurred any expense.

I wonder if anyone knows why we refer to our butts as fannies. The story is told of a man in the village saying at the store one day, "I'm going to go home and do something none of you can do. I'm going to go home and kiss my fanny." His wife was named Fanny.

For many Saturday nights when the children were young and television was also young, we had a ritual in our home. We ate hot dogs and drank Pepsi Cola sitting in front of the television as we watched the weekly episode of *Bonanza*. The hot dogs with potato chips were served in small baskets. It was always a cozy time and a fitting way to conclude the week. After many years *Pepsi and hot dogs* was shorthanded into "Phds." It sounded as if we had become cannibals! Even today when hot dogs are served we still say we are having Phds.

Tooky describes a time of broken relationships, disgruntlement, or discord in our family. "That was a tooky day," we might say. Sometimes the word is expanded to Tooky Turner—again, without any reason, logic, or reference. We make our apologies to the Turner families all over the world. If you were to hear someone say, "I am well *suffonsified*," you would think you had been dropped into a foreign world. This word is a creation of our own to explain being "stuffed to the gills" after a big meal.

About a year ago, upon leaving the Fox Theater after a Saturday matinee, I turned and said to the family, "Well, that was a real Jolly Roger," and they all shook their heads, affirming my assessment of the show we had just seen. If someone nearby had overheard what I'd said, they might have thought I was very pleased with the performance. However, they would have been totally wrong. When our children were very young, our best friends were Alvin and Mildred Caldwell. They were about our age and had a girl and a boy the ages of our children. The Caldwells and Hales played games together and also took vacations several times. It was on one of our vacation trips that the words *Jolly Roger* came into our vocabulary.

We journeyed to Daytona Beach for a week. Neither family had an abundance of funds, and the trip strained our budgets. On our last day, we decided to find the most exciting thing to do with the remainder of our cash. We had heard about a fabulous riverboat ride, which included seeing wildlife and a visit to an orange grove. We counted our funds and came up with the six dollars for each ticket. The captain of the boat—and only crew member—had a microphone and gave a guided tour down the river, pointing out alligators and deer, which we never saw. He chugged on down the river slowly enough for the mosquitoes to stay aboard and enjoy feasting on our blood. The sun got hotter and hotter, but we finally arrived at a dock and went ashore. There were orange trees, but we could not get close enough to them to take a picture. He brought ashore a large thermos of orange juice and paper cups and said, "Orange juice is fifty cents a cup." We just looked at him because we did not have the cash for it. He looked disappointed. Finally we returned to the starting place and went ashore.

The name of that boat was *Jolly Roger.* We knew we had been had, and Helen said, "I think we have been Jolly Rogered." That is the moment when Jolly Roger became our term for a downer. We began to laugh at the absurd way we had chosen to spend the last of our money. It had been a total washout.

When some aspiring word hawk does decide to compile into a dictionary words spoken "just at home," one word will be prominently displayed—and you can guess what word it is. It is the word *booger,* that nasty nose matter that is the gift of our sinus glands to all human beings. Many jokes about "boogers" filled my family's patter. Is the word local, regional, or universal? I doubt if there will ever be a doctoral dissertation written on the topic, but who "nose"?

VILLAGE

The Swing

FOR SOME REASON OR REASONS hidden in the deep well of my being, I keep finding myself sitting in the swing on the front porch of my boyhood home. There is no discernable trigger thought nor tangible reminder—it just happens. I am always alone when I return there, and it is morning time, cool and quiet except for background village sounds. The unpainted swing was made of oak slats, curved to fit your rump and back. The rhythmic tinkling ring each time the swing moved back and forth was part of the village background musical score. I can hear it now if I go there, as I often do.

Most of the time, as we lived in a house with ten other people, there would be three or more on the front porch, and the swing would be occupied. I loved it best when I had it all to myself, just me and my senses. It was my throne, from which I ruled the village. It was my mountain peak above the valley below and my place to sit and think about whatever it is young boys think about.

Returning there, I can taste the tartness of a green apple or a not-yet-ripe pear with its juice escaping down my chin. It is a sensation not readily duplicated in real time. If I am there in the early part of the morning, the smell of bacon frying and biscuits baking from several kitchens nearby fills the air with an "aroma" of peace and harmony. Life might be tough, resources meager, and relationships gone awry, but the smells of breakfast being prepared signaled "things are going to be all right."

From the swing I saw every car or truck that passed by. The cars were going places I would never go. I saw license plates from many faraway states—"Good gosh, that one is from Alabama!" Trucks carried things I would never have, puffing hard against the long hill they had to climb in front of our house. I didn't care where the cars were going or what the trucks carried, because during my swing moments I did not need anything.

From across the street a radio was turned up loud, blasting some gospel quartet's version of music into the morning air. The man on the porch smoked a cigarette and read the paper, his bare feet propped on the banister. He seemed the picture of contentment. Every once in a while, he folded the paper and joined in with the quartet, singing their way to Jesus.

When I return to that haven, I recall the spaciousness of our front porch. It was huge, twenty feet wide and seventy-five feet long in the mind of the boy in the swing, but in reality it was seven feet wide and about eighteen feet long. Just as that sort of dimensionality is exaggerated, so is the memory of the thoughts I had sitting there in the swing. My mind did not dwell on some massive thought, idea, ponderous question, or person in a book, because I never read a book. I did not question the universe or my place in it, because I did not wonder.

The swing moments were merely times for observation. They were moments to look, smell, and above all, listen to the village and house make their music—to let the world go by without evaluating it. It was just me, alone in the swing, at the center of the world, knowing this special time would not last very long. Soon enough someone would join me in the swing or a sound would break the mood: "Billy, where are you?" Mama needed something from the store or had not heard me in the past few minutes and thought I was into something that I should not be into. I could hear voices from inside the house but could not understand what they were saying except for an occasional loud: "I'm gonna tell Mama on you."

Admittedly, there were some moments when I was not alone in the swing. Sitting right beside me was my friend Worry. Worry was about the size of my Aunt Floridy, who was elephantine and stuck to us like glue. When she came to visit, she stayed and stayed like a bad cold, eating more than two or three of us put together would. She crowded our space. Worry was that way in the swing, pushing to get next to me, overly present in too many ways, and noisy.

Swing moments were times to see, hear, and smell—to feel the air swishing as the swing moved faster and higher, and faster still. Oh yes! There were those moments in which Worry rode with me. Times rehashed in my mind: how the preacher had described the end of the world and about some of us going to meet Jesus in the sky, or what Mama had said at breakfast about "making ends meet."

On a recent visit to Greenville, I had a strong desire to go back through the village to take a look at our house again. We drove up the street, and I stopped in front of the house. My, my! How small the house seemed to be! Boldly I went to the door and knocked, and when a resident came and opened the door, I said, "Ma'am, I hope you will not think I'm crazy, but I used to live here when I was a boy and just wanted to see the place. My wife and I spent the first few months of our marriage in that room." I pointed to one of the front bedrooms. "Could we just take a peek at that room?"

"It's a big mess in here right now," the occupant said, "but if you want to, come on in."

How small it seemed to be! There was no swing on the porch, but the two big hooks were still in the ceiling, and I wondered whether they were the originals. My swing now exists only in the echo chambers of my mind, but that's enough to help me create the many times I go back there.

Most of the time there I was surrounded by the rush of other people; our house pulsated with family and friends of all ages. People walked to and fro on the sidewalk in front of our house: old folks, children, some in groups, some by themselves, walking fast, walking slow, whistling or singing. The sidewalk was a busy place. "How you doing, Billy?" someone would shout. I would wave and keep on swinging. With all that going on, I still would be alone. Often our black cat, Honey, would come and sit on the banister of the porch cocking his—or her, no one knew—head from side to side as the swing followed its fixed path. Honey was a philosopher. That cat saw life as it was, never tried to improve it, but silently evaluated everything with cat wisdom. Honey was a wizard also, knowing everything you were thinking and smiling at your thoughts.

A windy day, with a bit of chill in the air, was the best of all times for a swing alone. Leaves would blow up on the porch and do their whirling dance before finding their settling-down place to await the broom, which would come to shove them on their way. The swish of a sudden breeze sounded like a bird flying too close. These minutes were hours and would live forever in the memory of the high-swinging boy.

In the background, the constant hum of the mill was a great comfort and served as the musical background of my swing moments. I have never found a place to be as peaceful as there in my "place alone." Our house was buzzing with voices, the radio and records playing for eighteen hours a day. Only from about midnight until five in the morning was there silence, except someone snoring or moving about to use the "slop jar." Moments of quiet, private time were rare, so I relished any time I could be alone in that squeaking, singing, humming swing. It was a retreat from the clamor and clutter of voices.

I was ten years into life, battered by fear of storms and death but bolstered by good food, movies, and love. I tolerated school. I hated church. I loved my movies and the taste of popcorn. I was enchanted with the records my brother bought for our new Victrola phonograph and learned to sing along with them. I was intrigued by relatives from Lyman, Piedmont, and Pelzer. In every way, I was just a regular little boy who lived in the "now," and the best place to do that was in the front-porch swing all my myself.

"Dinner's ready!" someone yells down the long hall and suddenly I am back in the world of others. When I leave the swing with a big jump, it keeps on moving back and forth, singing its squeaky music, slowly and more slowly, its last just-audible word: "Come back some time."

Doodle, Monk, and Me

BREAKFAST AT OUR HOUSE WAS a cup of coffee with milk and sugar stirred in and a couple of Mama's marvelous biscuits crumbled into the coffee. This was the tradition in Mama's family, who loved to "eat their coffee." In the summer weeks of no school before I became a teenager, I could lie in bed long past school's morning time. I slept with my face toward the sun and old sol would rise, massaging my face with brilliance. I would rub the sleep from my eyes, stretch and yawn, take off my gown, slide into the clothes that were lying on the floor where I'd left them last night, and go toward the kitchen. The four grownups, my two older sisters and two older brothers, would have eaten but left us some biscuits. Mama would be on the front porch stringing beans, peeling potatoes, or reading the morning paper. The house would be morning cool and quiet.

While my little sisters slept more, I would eat my coffee, my mind in high gear. What does a twelve-year-old boy think about that early? What thoughts roamed around in my head? I certainly did not have to plan my day, because most of my days were without an agenda; the hours just happened, one after the other, without anything to distinguish one from the other. There was no schedule to anticipate and nothing to do except whatever happened. There is much truth in the stirring song from the recent Broadway musical *Big River*, which has a line saying that a boy must grow up to be a man but "Only once in his life is he free." When I woke on those long-ago mornings, I was free.

In early July 1937, things would be different. As I ate my coffee, my mind idled somewhere—maybe it was about school, where just a few weeks ago, on my final report card, the word *retained* had been written. I did not know the word, but I guessed it did not mean promoted. I had failed the fifth grade. But I doubt that preyed on my mind that day. I might have been thinking about selling candy, which was my chief occupation at the time, or it could have been finding the morning paper and checking to see how many hits Lou Gehrig had gotten the day before. I was a member in good standing of the Lou Gehrig Fan Club, with a pen to wear and a baseball card to brag about. The New York Yankees was the team I pulled for.

When I came down the center hall that morning after breakfast, headed for the front porch, I heard Mama talking to Mrs. Bishop, who lived next door and who had an abundant vegetable garden. She had seen Mama on the porch and brought her a handful of red tomatoes. I walked out without speaking and sat down on the steps. The sun rose on the back of the house, making the front steps the cool place to be at this time.

My no-agenda day was about to change in a big way. I saw Doodle Thomas coming around the corner of the village gymnasium, where his office was located, and he seemed to be heading in our direction. He was the athletic director for the village, husband of the pianist at the church, graduate of Clemson College, and stellar long-shot artist on the basketball court, but most of all he was a friend to Mama. I knew he always let Mama, and whoever happened to be with her, get in free at the baseball and basketball games. It was his way of helping out. He was a young man, much younger than Mama, but they kidded each other when they met at church or passed each other at the company store. Doodle often hired me to deliver circulars announcing the sports event of the week. He printed them in his office. They were just single sheets, usually on green paper. "Put one on every porch," he would say, emphasizing the word *every*. There were more than two hundred houses in our village. Each time it took me most of the day, unless I convinced my little sisters to help me. He paid me a quarter, and if they helped I would buy them a sack of penny candy at the drugstore.

This morning, Doodle came to the corner and yelled, "Billy, come here a minute." I naturally thought he had circulars to be delivered. As I approached where he stood, I noticed he had no circulars in his hand. He said, "Would you like to go to camp for a week?"

"Yes, sir."

"Well, go get packed! You have to be at the YMCA, uptown, by eleven o'clock to catch the bus—I'll call Monk and tell him you are coming, Don't be late."

Monk Mulligan was the director of Greenville's YMCA and a friend of Doodle's. He had called him that morning because he had a vacancy for one more boy at Camp Greenville for the week; he hoped the Dunean Mill folks could supply a boy and pick up the costs. I was the one selected to go. It was near Hendersonville, North Carolina, and boys from all over the South came there for a week to this first-class camp run by the YMCA.

My brother had a small athletic bag he used for his basketball uniform when the team traveled; that was the only thing we had to use for packing my camp clothes. I packed an extra pair of pants and another shirt, a towel, a bar of soap, and a pair of swimming trunks my brother never used anymore. That's all I carried for the week. I had never done this before!

There was no discussion about *where* I was going—all we knew was that I was to meet Monk at the YMCA uptown—nor did I have any idea when I would be back, until Mama said, "You want to go to camp for a week? Go up and tell Emmer you are going to camp this week."

Emmer was pleased I was going to camp. She said, "You will need a little spending money," and she gave me a dollar bill. I think that was what Mama had in mind; she probably had no cash herself.

With my bag in hand and my dollar in my pocket, I caught the trolley, but not before I turned and waved bye to Mama and two of my little sisters who were standing on the front porch. When I got uptown, I hurried to the YMCA as fast as I could walk.

Out front of the YMCA there was a bunch of well-dressed boys about my size. They all had suitcases and wore some kind of caps that were all alike. There was a big blue bus out front for us to load into and start this adventure. I walked up to Monk Mulligan. I recognized him from his visits to our village to watch his old buddy play basketball. "You must be Billy!" he said with a big smile.

I never signed a paper nor did I register or tell anybody my full name. I remained "Billy" all week. The only instructions given were, "Load up, boys." Monk drove the bus with about fifteen boys and a couple of college men who were camp assistants on board. All those boys with the black caps on were from the YMCA in Miami, Florida, and they knew each other. I felt a little strange, out of place, and a sudden weepy feeling of homesickness possessed me. They sang songs that I did not know, but I soon caught on and sang with them. Several buses loaded with boys had left other YMCAs around the region. When they all got there, about 150 boys were in the camp.

I was assigned to the cabin with the boys from Miami. The first thing I noticed was that they had billfolds with several dollar bills, and they unpacked their suitcases into the footlockers at the ends of our cots. I put my whole athletic bag down in my footlocker. My dollar bill stayed in my pocket. They chatted and teased each other, and I felt left out. Their names were strange ones: Josh, Jerry, Michael, and Logan. These were unlike the boys names back in the village: Lard, Stein, Wadd, Hunky, and Ob.

The "big house" at the camp was a combination dining hall, gymnasium, chapel, and snack bar. Soon after arriving we heard a huge gong, which filled the whole valley. It was the call to come to the dining hall. We lined up, holding our trays, while some black ladies spooned food onto them. My, my! What good food—and huge servings. I was beginning to feel better about saying "yes, sir" to Doodle. Swimming and hiking filled each afternoon, and then it was back to that glorious dining hall. After supper we went to vespers. I had never heard the word before. It was a religious time, with singing, and Monk spoke every time, saying things about how God had made all the things in nature for us to enjoy. In the back of the little hymn book there was a song we sang each night and another word I had never heard: *doxology*. This was nothing like church back home.

The first night, at ten o'clock, someone with a bugle played "taps," and then the grownups shouted, "Lights out." I hadn't planned on this. I had never slept in a dark house. Mama always kept a light on in the hall. The lights went out, my heart raced, and I strained to see. Slowly the stars and night sky became visible through the wire-screened windows at the top of the cabin. What a relief!

Before breakfast one morning, early in the week, one of the Miami boys said, "Hey, Billy, I got an extra cap. You want to wear it this week?" I hopped at the offer; it would make me a little like them. All week the routines were three good meals a day, snack bar open after lunch, swimming, crafts, hikes, games, and vespers. After breakfast we went to *devotional*, another word I had never heard, sang songs like "When Morning Gilds the Sky" and "O, Worship the King"—not like those back home, "There's Power in the Blood" or "Just as I Am." I liked this kind of church.

As the days moved on, the Miami boys proved to be friendly, and they included me in their chatter and free-time activities. One evening midweek there came a fierce storm, with big wind and lightning. I was anxious and scared, but they did not give it a thought except to say after a big roar of thunder, "Boy! That one was a big one!" and then all laugh. I was experiencing a storm without being in the "nut house" back home, where a storm was as scary as the Second Coming promised so often at church. I had been raised with great fear of storms, thanks to my oldest sister, who was morbidly afraid of the elements. I had caught my unusual fear of lightning and thunder from her. A storm outside created even more of a storm inside our house!

The announcement was made on Thursday that on Friday night we would all go over the mountain for a party and dance at the girls' camp. Added to that announcement was the instruction "and plan to wear some long pants." A dance? Were they sure that *C* in YMCA meant "Christian"? I had an advantage. My sister Louise and I had danced some at home, so I at least knew what to do. I had no long pants to wear as they suggested. One of the Miami boys sensed my dilemma and let me borrow a pair of his. The pants were wrinkled pretty badly, so I straightened them out and put them under my mattress to press them for the dance.

We went across the mountain on Friday night after supper to the girls' camp. They were all dressed up and looked pretty, like my sisters on Sunday mornings. At first we square-danced, or at least tried to. I got into it fairly well, more so than the Miami boys, who bragged on me, which gave me confidence to try even harder. I felt successful! Later, there was some "shore 'nuff" dancing, and I asked a girl to dance. We danced, but she was very uncomfortable and wanted to stop before the music was finished. For the last dance we formed two huge circles, one inside the other. The girls were on the inside and the boys on the outside, and the circles moved in opposite directions. When the music stopped, as it did often, we were to turn and shake hands with the girls standing next to us. It was a lot of fun. What would my preacher think of me, up here in the hills, dancing?

Most of the boys received a letter from home during the week. They talked about buying something from the craft store to take home to their parents. I did not get any mail. Mama did not even know where I was, and I had no money to buy anything. My snack dollar had run out on Thursday. One of the camp workers saw me not standing in line at the snack bar. "Billy, you out of money?" he asked.

I told him I was, and he gave me a dime. I thanked him, and for the rest of the week we were smiling buddies.

On Sunday morning we had a full-blown worship service with a preacher from a nearby church. He was funny and made me feel good. He talked about going to camp when he was a boy and getting homesick and crying. This did not feel like church at all. We loaded up the bus and came back to the YMCA. When we got off the bus, nearly all of the Miami boys came and shook my hand, saying things like "Good to meet you" and "Hope to see you next year." We had had a week of fun together. I rode home on the trolley and surprised Mama. She did not know when I would be back. My week at camp was over except for lingering thoughts.

My little sisters, Mama, and my two brothers wanted me to tell them about what I had done at camp. I told them some stories about the food, the Miami boys, and the dance, but I could not tell them other things, because it would be some time before I could gather my thoughts and put them in order.

I went to camp as a charity case from Depression poverty, thrown in with middle-class boys whose families had enough money to send them to a very fine North Carolina camp, and I survived.

I got to eat three big meals a day of the best food I had ever tasted and a candy bar every day, sometimes two.

I went to church that was warm and fun, bright and smiling, without an invitation hymn that lasted for an eternity.

I cast a personality there that was aggressive, fun-filled, and free from judgments—a future was born that week.

I had to cover my deficiency of resources and experiences by being a leader and treating everybody as a friend. I had to be more than I was.

Thanks to Doodle and Monk, a boy got a glimpse of what he could do if he took charge.

The village, my house, my family, and my friends were the same when I returned. I was not, but they did not know it yet. It is sometimes best to hold your "newness" until a time when you are ready to use it.

"My God, Here Comes Argo!"

ONE BRIGHT SPRING MORNING SEVERAL years ago, our daughter, Kathy, ran into the house very distraught, shouting, "Bootsey is dead! My Bootsey is dead." Bootsey had been her most delightful cat among the three cats who had roamed our yard for four or five years. She had originally found Bootsey under the gingko tree in the corner of our front yard where she now lay dead. She had been an abandoned little kitty, shivering, frightened, and mewing in a small desperate voice when Kathy found her. She had been afraid of us, but we finally coaxed the kitty toward us with a lid of milk.

Kathy cried more and more because she'd had a very special attachment to Bootsey. She led me out in the yard and pointed to the cat. I saw the lump of black fur, but we did not walk very close to the scene. I assured her we would bury Bootsey when we returned from our morning walk. She was satisfied when I told her we would bury her right on the same spot where she had found her as a scared baby kitty. I hated that duty; no one knows how I disliked it! There was, however, a special feature to this death. Bootsey had instinctively gone back to die in the place we'd found her.

On returning from our walk, Kathy and I got the shovel and went to the scene. Bootsey was a black-and-white cat. Taking the shovel, I turned her over to move her so we could bury her in the exact spot where she'd died, and I dug a hole. We held hands and then made prayer hands.

"Will Bootsey go to heaven?" Kathy asked.

"Yes! Bootsey was a good cat," I said.

We buried Bootsey there and covered the gravesite with a pile of pine needles.

"Can I get another cat?"

"We sure will, as soon as we can find one."

Secretly I was hoping Bootsey's death would mean one less cat in our lives, not because we were in mourning but because—well, to be honest—we never delighted in any household pet. Members of the larger family believed us to be neglectful toward most of the cats and dogs we had as pets, who had names like Precious, Patch, Professor, Black Beauty, Lumberjack, Chic Filet, and Old Gray Boy.

That afternoon we were sitting in the family room, reading. Kathy, looking out the window, shouted, "Bootsey's not dead! Bootsey's not dead. She's right there in the backyard!"

We ran to the window. There was Bootsey, walking up the steps. Kathy ran out and hugged her, weeping tears of joy. I looked at Helen and said, "Whose cat did we bury, and where did it come from?" That mystery was never solved. I had grown up with cats and other animal life but really did not want them in my house when I became head of a household. In my boyhood days I had been surrounded by "all creatures great and small"—very, very small ones included.

Animals and animal life were prominent in the lives of the people of the village and especially at our house. We, like all families, had flies in the house because our garbage cans, with no lids, were out in the back alley not far from our house and contained all of the household garbage. These cans bred flies by the thousands. In the summer months, before the dinner and supper meals we would have a "fly shooing." Several members of the family would take either a towel or a newspaper, line up in one end of the house and shoo the flies toward one door, which was opened just at the precise moment all the fly shooers got there, releasing a swarm of flies. It was a good way to rid the house of most of the flies, for a while, at least. When we could afford it, Mama would buy a Flit gun and spray, which was helpful but stunk up the house.

Another pesky tiny animal that lived with us from time to time was the notorious bed bug. These were sneaky little things that lived in the nooks and folds of our mattresses and came out only at night. They were vampirish, sucking the blood out of us by burying their heads in our skin. Frequently we had to take our mattresses outside and clean the nooks and seams with kerosene in order to kill them and their eggs.

At school we came in contact with yet another member of the animal kingdom, head lice. I've mentioned before Mama's kerosene cure for these.

A constant battle was waged against a slightly larger animal, the cockroach. Old Noah should have been buggy whipped for taking this nastiest of all the small creatures with him on the Ark of legend.

The presence of flies, bed bugs, lice, and mice was not evidence of neglect nor nasty hygiene habits. They were part of the condition of life in those days. Personal and public hygiene were not as easily maintained then as they are currently, clear evidence that government-established public health standards have changed how we live. The conditions in which I grew up are still present, but only in the most impoverished areas of the country.

We always had cats when I was growing up; nearly every family had a cat or two. It was the only way to control the mouse population. The dominance of cats and their propensity to procreate indiscriminately meant that cats were ever present. However, there were a few special pets in the village other than cats.

The Davis family had a little rat terrier they named Trixy because it could walk on its hind legs and go to the couch and act as if it were praying. There was Lila Hart, an eccentric old maid from the mill office who had a parrot named Polly, which she said could say ten words. But when she had Polly demonstrate for us its talent, all of the words sounded like "hakkoy." However, in order to please her, we acted as if we had heard real words, which was a guarantee to get us each a cookie from her cookie jar.

Old Rob, who worked in the back room of the company store, was in charge of killing and dressing all the chickens for the butcher. Old Rob was a gray-haired black man with only a couple of teeth, who told us tales of the village folks. He knew which men in the village were members of the Ku Klux Klan and where they hid their robes, but he would not tell us their names. Rob had a huge tarantula spider he had found in a bunch of bananas. He kept it in a little cage and fed it insects, and he would scare us with it as a practical joke.

I never had a dog of my own to keep me company or to train to retrieve a stick, but we had cats: live-in cats; cats with black fur; cats who sat by the fire and purred; cats who played with mice, taunting them until they made the sudden kill; cats who sat majestically in the windows as if they were nobility. There was a long line of cats, several generations of them, all named Honey. They roamed through the house, ignoring us as they made their way to another spot to pose. Those cats picked their friends among the family members as carefully as the iceman chose which families could get ice and pay at the end of the week and which had to pay upon delivery of the ice. My brother George was never chosen as a friend of any of the Honeys, because he hated cats and kicked them out of his way and never allowed one to sit on his lap in front of the fire. We had cats who, when in a romantic mood, wailed like crying babies from under our house, especially late at night. I remember asking Mama what that noise was, and she said, "They just tomcatting around." It seemed like every time, after a night of wailing and crying, later there would be a new litter of little Honeys. Occasionally, a Honey would jump up on the table when it was set with our supper meal, causing someone to shout, "I'm gonna kill that cat someday."

A few families had dogs, mostly good dogs who stayed in their yards but patrolled their territory diligently to keep stray cats on the run.

Animals added to the drama of village life in significant ways. The mill company provided two locations, just off the village, where folks could keep a cow or a pig. These places were referred to as the "cow pasture" and "pig pens." It was a common sight to see people headed toward the cow pasture with a big pail filled with bread scraps from their table to feed the pig, or to see someone coming from there carrying a pail of fresh milk. Some of the people in the village who couldn't quite leave the farm totally had chicken pens in their yards, which provided them with eggs and an occasional Sunday dinner. If you lived close by one of these houses, a rooster called the sun up every day just for you.

The village animals were unlike those on the farm; they did no work. They were toys to be enjoyed, simply a part of the picturesque scenery. Some families loved their cats or dogs as if they were members of the family, including them in activities like a Sunday afternoon ride in the mountains. We were amused at the Donnan family, who lived behind us, because of the way they worshipped their beautiful solid-white Persian cat. We were eating dinner one day when we heard people wailing and moaning. It was the Donnans walking around in shock and hugging each other. They had just discovered their cat had been smashed under the wheels of the ice truck. That afternoon, when Mr. Donnan came home from work, the whole family gathered at the edge of their corn patch. Mrs. Donnan was carrying a well-decorated box containing the dead cat. Their teenage son, R. W., brought a shovel and dug a big grave in which they placed the box. Then they all stood and held hands for a while, in a ceremony of some kind, dedicated to praying that cat into cat heaven, I suppose.

Our Honeys died most of the time by being smashed under the wheels of transfer trucks that regularly passed in front of our house on US Highway 29. When a Honey died, we simply got another one. The village trash men would pick up any animals that died. We had no burials or ceremonies, nor did we grieve. A cat had simply died!

For a very short time we had a little dog. The dog of my sister's friend had a litter of puppies, and she gave us one. It had no tail, a birth defect. We named it No Tail Hale. It was not welcomed by Honey and disappeared one day. We never saw it again. No Tail Hale probably sensed that we were cat people and joined the circus.

Normally the pets of other families did not bother us, but there was one exception to the rule. The name *Argo* lives vividly in infamy in the minds and hearts of all who knew him. That name still causes me to shudder with anxiety. Argo! There never was another animal like that one in the history of the village.

The Garren boys, who lived across the street from us, brought the puppy back from a trip to North Carolina. That puppy had the biggest feet I had ever seen on a dog—huge feet, each nearly the size of its head.

People from all over the village came to see this frisky little puppy. It was a cute little dog. It would jump up on you and try to chew at your pants leg. Argo was a full-blooded Great Dane, and as he grew he became stronger and stronger. He would chase us, knock us down, and go for our socks. That dog had a thing about socks. His teeth would grab your socks and tear them until they ripped off. For a little while it was entertaining, but as he got bigger and bigger it became less and less fun.

Soon they had to build a fence to contain him. Contain Argo? Forget it! He had grown to his full size and was as big as a small donkey. The first fenced-in area they built lasted about four hours. He tore it down and parked himself on their front porch. They put him on a leash and tied it to a porch post, which he nearly pulled from its footing. The second dog pen they built was much stronger, but he climbed over it or jumped over it. Then they built it higher, until it was ten feet high. When they tried to take him for a walk on the leash, he dragged them along, going wherever he wanted to go. This was a big, strong dog! What started out as a cute little puppy who chewed our socks was now the terror of the village, a menace to the citizenry, and a beast feared by children, adults, and every animal, large and small.

To pacify Argo, the butcher at the meat counter of the company store supplied the Garrens with huge bones from which he had taken the meat. Some of them were a foot long. It was awesome to stand and watch Argo take a bone and toss it around in his enclosure, then start chewing and growling. As long as he had a bone, we were all safe from him committing some dastardly deed. When this donkey-sized dog barked, it sounded like a ship's foghorn. We lived across the street from the Garren family. We could see the ten-foot-high dog pen from our front porch, and if Argo was standing up at the fence, as he usually did, we could see his huge head looking at us, curious and menacing.

One Sunday afternoon our relatives from Piedmont, who were my Papa's brother's widow and children, came to visit us. They had driven up to see us often since Papa had died, to give moral support to Mama and us from the larger Hale family. This particular Sunday was in the middle of summer, and we were all sitting under the sycamore tree in our front yard. That majestic old tree, the prettiest in the whole village, cast its shadow all over the yard. Sitting in the circle that day were the grand dame of the Piedmont Hales, Aunt Fanny, as prim and proper as Queen Victoria; her son, Dick Hale; her daughter, Bernice; and her new husband, Mr. D. J. Luther. Long before the word was invented, he was a *nerd*. He had on his Sunday coat and tie, shoes shined to flashpoint, and on his head he wore a gray fedora. He sat straight up with grand posture, moving very little, and his face was frozen in a manikin-like stare. He worked in the office at the mill in Piedmont and carried the air of a man gifted in self-adoration.

At some point, Mama suggested that some of the boys go over to the drugstore, which was only about a hundred yards away, and buy us all ice-cream cones. My brother and I took orders: Mr. Luther ordered vanilla, which suited his character and demeanor; others wanted chocolate, strawberry, or tutti-frutti. Aunt Fanny gave us the money to buy the ice creams. No one objected, because she was known for her significant resources and generosity. We rushed back so the ice cream would not melt. It was cool and refreshing and a perfect moment on a leisurely Sunday afternoon as we licked our cones and told family stories, new and old. Into this peaceful moment, all of a sudden, we heard Mr. Garren shout at the top of his voice, "Come back here, Argo!"

What a waste of breath.

Argo, who was stone deaf to commands, galloped across the street at Argo speed, with his big feet pounding the ground like a horse. My sister ran up on the front porch, shouting, "My God, here comes Argo!"

I climbed up the chinaberry tree and hollered, "Argo got out—Argo got out!"

Everybody scattered toward whatever could serve as shelter from the beast on the chase, except for Mr. D. J. Luther, who sat frozen in place, with his ice-cream cone in his hand resting on the arm of the chair. Argo set that ice-cream cone as his target, making one pass by Mr. D. J. Luther, gulping down that cone in one swallow and, in the passing, bumping Mr. D. J. Luther's chair leg. This caused him to fall backward—at which time his fedora fell off, exposing to all the fact that he did not have a hair on his head. He grabbed his hat and quickly placed it back on his head, watching in horror as that galloping modern dinosaur hunted more. Mr. D. J. Luther was humiliated. Argo made a wide turn around the chairs, seeking feverishly for another treat. Mama was hiding behind the trunk of the sycamore tree but made the mistake of not hiding her cone of chocolate ice cream. The beast took it out of her hand on the run. Argo then sat down on the sidewalk so he could look over the scene for more delectables.

Mr. Garren approached the dog, placed a leash on him, and followed as Argo pulled him back across the street toward their house. He yelled back apologies for the storm that Argo had caused at our ice-cream party. We gathered back in the circle with our company from Piedmont and began to laugh at the crazy scene in which we had all been principal actors—all, that is, except Mr. D. J. Luther, who was by that time sitting in the driver's seat of their car, looking straight ahead, ready to make his escape from the chaos and the village.

"I think D. J. is ready to go," his wife said.

The Piedmont relatives came back a few more times, but we never saw the bald-headed Mr. D. J. Luther again.

A few weeks passed, and Argo was sold to a man in Piedmont. We never saw him again, but we can still hear great stories as told by the older folks about the Argo era in the village. Word came to us later that cousin Bernice and her husband, Mr. D. J. Luther, had moved to Virginia. What about that?

"Billy, Where You Been?"

Never underestimate the power in any one moment
of time, because therein may lie the fibers from
which you can weave the fabric of life someday.

I T WAS DURING THE FIRST few weeks of a lifetime of school, and like many days before, Mama let me walk up the back alley by myself to meet Papa, who walked home from work right after five o'clock each day. I was six years old and in the first grade. He was the new paymaster at the mill. Papa was tall as a tree and chubby like Santa Claus, with a smile as wide as the ocean, and he was sweeter than summer watermelon.

"Papa, I made 100 in spelling today, and tomorrow I'm going to make 110!"

He bent over and picked me up, hugged me tight, and said, "Shore 'nuff?" Then he put me down, and we walked hand in hand, his big hand swallowing my little hand, back down the alley and in the back door of our house. He walked in telling the family, "My Billy made 100 on spelling today and tomorrow he is going to make 110."

They all got a good laugh and I was proud. Was this the beginning of my journey into elaborating on a truth—better known as telling stories?

One of the quirks of the human mind is how it selects which things to keep on the top shelf and which ones to put somewhere deep in mind space, making it difficult to retrieve. I can remember nearly all of my elementary school teachers' names but not a single thing they taught me. Embedded in my mental profile, each of those teachers had one characteristic that serves as a mental marker to help me remember them.

I might remember them doing, saying, or being a certain something, but still I cannot recall anything I learned specifically from any one of them.

My first-grade teacher, Miss Pyron, gently scolded me one morning when she noticed that I had come to school from a different direction. She questioned me, "Where do you live, Billy?"

I said, "On Allen Street."

"Did you move?"

"Yes, ma'am"

"Well, we have to know where you live. Are you sure you moved?"

"Yes, ma'am"

I felt bad about that and told Mama. She wrote a note for me to take the next day.

In the second grade, my teacher was Miss Young. We were having a class play for the students, who brought a penny for admission, and I was selected to collect the money. There was a lull in folks coming, so I decided to start counting our money. I remember what she said: "Don't count the money until the show is over."

My third-grade teacher left no mark at all for me to remember her by, not even her name. However, deep down I know I must have learned many things during those long days of hours.

Miss Abroms was next in the parade of early teachers. She was tall, redheaded, and not pretty. One day, one of the girls was bending too far over a table and showing her panties, and Miss Abroms said to me, "Billy, go tell Dot to pull her dress down." I did not do it. What crazy things we remember from past times!

This teacher, Miss Abroms, was my fifth-grade teacher. I failed this grade because I did not understand fractions and was battling hallucinations caused by not dealing effectively with the grief of my Papa's death. Who can get with fractions when his mind is obsessed with the radical fear of storms, the threat of hellfire from the church, and mental illness?

My successful run at fifth grade the next year was with Miss Warner, and here again I draw a blank except for the time she whipped me with a rubber tube for missing sixteen out of twenty spelling words on the weekly Friday spelling test.

Julia Foster was my sixth-grade teacher, and all I remember about her were the many afternoons after school when she came and sat with Mama on the front porch in the swing. They seemed to like each other. Mama made them glasses of iced tea, and they talked for a long time, but I never knew what they talked about. Was it me, perhaps?

Then came the seventh grade, and here time seemed to stand still for a while. My life took on a different color, a new song, and a new rhythm. It seemed that all of a sudden school became a neat place to be. There was, of course, a cause for this transformation. Her name was Ruth Stevens. She was a tall, stately woman, with deep-blue eyes that did not simply look at your eyes but hooked you into hers. She had blonde hair, which was positioned at the sides of her head in pre-Raphaelite coils. When she walked around the room, it was if she floated; the room seemed to move with her. Ruth Stevens was always present in the space where she walked, never disjointed or flustered. She was a great pod of energy. To be in her world was to be comfortable and secure.

Ruth Stevens was unlike all the women of our village, including Mama. The village women were sagging from having had too many children over too short a period of time. They were sallow, worn out, and often lacking an uplifting spirit because their world consisted of work, work, and more work, often footnoted with work in the evenings. The women were often sad because life seemed to be going no place. Not Ruth Stevens! She stood in stark contrast to the village women. She wore starched dresses that emitted a fragrance, fresh and clean, a fragrance you cannot duplicate today, because nobody knows how to make starch with that fragrance anymore. With her I was unwittingly establishing values that would manifest themselves much later in life, but I did not know it then.

Very early in the year, before I had a chance to know Miss Stevens very well, I came in a bit late one morning. We were known as the "late Hales." The other students were already at work in their workbooks. The school system in our village was "progressive education," patterned after the experimental schools of John Dewey in Chicago. We never sat at desks, including throughout high school. We had tables with seats for six students. Each place had a nice cubbyhole for workbooks. That morning

I quietly went to my table, took out my workbook, and quickly went into my stare. I stared most of the time in the days after Papa had died. It was a Tuesday. It had to be a Tuesday. Have you ever noticed Tuesday? It has nothing going for it; it has no redeeming qualities. Somewhere back in time, they put in Tuesday just to separate Monday and Wednesday. Tuesdays are very long and slow passing. Just like all school days. It was a Tuesday!

I was in my stare, but I always knew where Ruth Stevens was in the room. It was as if I had some kind of radar. That morning she stood in the far corner of the room for a while, looking over the class. Then, slowly, she walked down past the bulletin boards on China that we had put up with meticulous detail. She came to the windows. It was an October Tuesday; hot and cold were still battling to see who would win. In my mind, I sensed her walking past the windows and the hissing radiators and stopping at the pencil sharpener. She stood there, still and quiet, for a minute or two. Then she came to my table, like a gentle wind; she just blew gently into my world. I knew she was near because I smelled the fragrance of the starch in her dress. And then she knelt down beside me, crackling and crinkling that starched dress as she went down, each crackle or crinkle releasing a burst of that starch. She turned her face toward mine, and I turned my face in to hers. Our eyes hooked into each other's, and time deepened into memory.

Then she whispered into my sails, "Billy, where have you been?"

Quick as a wink I said, "Home with Mama."

Then she asked with great tenderness, "Was it fun?"

Even quicker, I said, "Yes, ma'am."

In the next moment the most unbelievable thing occurred. Ruth Stevens stood up, top tall, and floated away like the wind, on her rounds about the room. She did not stand up and yell back at me: "But pay attention!" No! She simply walked away, and in that moment she gave dignity to my reverie and planted a seed, which grew to be the foundation for a life of relating to others.

It has taken me through the graying of these decades to find that moment and revisit it. Something had to be there, for why else would I, through the years, have spent so much time trying to give other people the space to be who they needed to be at a particular moment?

Ruth Stevens must have heard from someone that my brother George had bought the family a new electric record player to replace the old Grafonola, the type you had to crank up for it to play. One day, at the end of the school day, she asked me to come by her desk before I left. Naturally, I thought she wanted to suggest some way I could improve my scholarship or deportment. She reached in a drawer, handed me a record album containing four records, and said, "Play these. There is a surprise in them."

On the way home I read the cover; it said, *William Tell Overture*, by Rossini. I did play it, waiting for the surprise, which finally came on the last record. It was the theme of the radio show *The Lone Ranger*. I was thrilled! The whole family listened to it. The next day I took the album back and thanked her, telling her I had found the surprise. This was my quiet introduction to classical music. A master teacher was at work.

About a month later, the scene was nearly replicated. She handed me another record album. "Billy," she said, "this one will interest you." It was Edvard Grieg's *Peer Gynt Suite*. The first side was "At Dawn." It did sound like morning. The second side was "Anitra's Dance," a very pretty tune. Then came "The Hall of the Mountain King," a rousing, powerful full-orchestra number. The last was "The Storm." Imagine, a storm in music! It was both exciting and soothing. I was in a storm, and it did not frighten me. What did Ruth know? Was all this merely coincidental, or was this again a top-flight professional teacher at work? Every student deserves at least one teacher who turns him or her on to life.

Frederick Beuchner says, "Listen to your life. You are happening— now. These moments we are living are not a dress rehearsal for later. This is life ... listen!" Listen or you might miss the Ruths who come so infrequently in our journeys.

I don't know where Ruth Stevens went when she left at the end of that year, but I bet she was always looking for another Billy to help launch on a new adventure. She lives in me even as I tell this story. I can still hear her saying, "Billy, where you been?"

Watering the Ferns:
A Story from On High

NATURE DID A FINE PIECE of masterwork when it designed the big chinaberry tree that dominated our backyard. It was made for climbing. Limbs on the tree were spaced exactly so I could grab one, swing up, grab the next higher one, and shinny to the top in seconds. In the top of the tree, three branches made a comfortable nest from which I could see into the backyards of ten houses. That nest was "my place" during all the years of my boyhood. During the summer months there was thick foliage to hide me away, which made for even more privacy. The villagers and my family could not see me, but I could see them.

I watched the washerwomen hanging clothes on the line, the garbage men emptying cans onto their truck, and neighbors digging and harvesting in their gardens. I could hear people talking but could not hear what they were saying, except when there was a heated exchange between husbands and wives. Being there in my place gave me the sensation of making a movie of village life. A boy needs a place he can go and cogitate about life, to let his mind idle awhile and go from thought to thought without a plan or a worry. My place in the lofty top of that chinaberry tree was where I could go and just be "boy." Looking down on lonely rooftops was interesting. Some had odd objects on top of them, such as newspapers that had been tossed too high by the paper boy. There was one roof with a huge rock on it, and I wondered how it had gotten there. Pity the boy who has no place of his own where he can go and do nothing, slowly, dwelling deep in the present, oblivious of the past or the future. There were many times during the winter months when I was sitting in school wishing I was in my nest, away from that thing called spelling.

Under each of those lonely looking roofs was a story, a family, a history, and people. Often there were three generations living in a house. All of the families had their own characteristics: the McDonalds were a very quiet family; the Grubbs played their radio loud enough for the neighbors to enjoy; the Donnans loved to sit in their yard in the chairs Mr. Donnan had made in his workshop; the Colemans were Methodist; the Harmons were childless; and the Lukewires were "green people," which meant they had just come to the village from the farm. The Williams family had a Model A Ford, which they washed frequently. This was interesting to watch because their teenage daughter helped, and she wore shorts. I liked that.

I also observed my own family from my perch on high. It was from here that I sometimes watched Mama on a Saturday come out of the back door and sit down on the steps to let the sun dry her hair. Sometimes she hummed some tune of comfort but sometimes she just stared into the yard. As she combed her long tresses, which normally were in a bun on the back of her head, I wondered what she was thinking and hoped it was not about Papa dying.

Mondays were wash day in the village and black women came by the dozens, walking up the back alleys to their jobs. I liked to be in my place high above the yards, when all the clothes were hung on the clotheslines, especially if there was a stiff wind blowing. The wind would make the clothes sing their *snap-flap-hum* song. With all those clothes singing in the wind, yard after yard, it looked like an ocean of waves. At times my nest was a truly magical place!

Of all the characters within view of my nest, the family next door, the Drakes, were the most fascinating to watch. There were four in the family, headed by Mrs. Drake, who was ancient of days and long of tooth. She wore a bonnet obviously made from flour-sack cloth. I never saw her without her bonnet. Mrs. Drake had a middle-aged daughter, Ruby, who worked in the mill and walked so slowly she appeared to be a figure in a still-life painting. Also living there were twin men who were long past middle age, Ike and Ark. They were tall, skinny, bony men who wore bib overalls constantly. They had not worked in years, if ever. The chief occupation of Ike and Ark was to sit on their back steps, carefully roll cigarettes, light them from one match, and smoke, blowing smoke rings in the air, while never speaking a word to each other. Their hobby was watering their mama's ferns. Mrs. Drake was known village-wide for her green thumb. Her corn was the biggest and greenest from any garden in our block and would have won a blue ribbon at the county fair. She had five huge potted ferns sitting on the edge of their storm cellar. They had dug a storm cellar many years before. It looked like a big mound of grass, except for the door going into the cellar. They were the only family in the village with a storm cellar.

Ike and Ark spent an unusual amount of time watering those ferns. Their routine, a couple of times a day was this: one of them, Ike or Ark, would come outside, go down in the storm cellar to get a small jar, take it to the outside faucet, fill it with water, put a little on each fern, take the jar back down to the storm cellar and, after a short time, come up, close the door, and slowly meander back into the house. I observed, from my nest, this process being accomplished regularly each day. It was strange behavior, but then they were a strange bunch.

Near dusk one evening, I was coming home from R. W. Donnan's house, cutting through the neighbors' gardens, when I saw one of the twins, I could not tell which one, descend into the storm cellar carrying two large bottles of water, or I assumed it was water. As I got closer, I said, "Ark (I had guessed right), you watering the ferns?" He looked around, mumbled something, and descended back into the storm cellar.

That night might not have remained in my memory bank except for what happened next. I stopped, picked up a green pear, and quickly climbed up the chinaberry tree into my nest with the pear in my pocket. I could eat it there because Mama would not see me and say, "You eat a green pear at night it will kill you." That night I was willing to take a chance. I sat there in my place, eating my pear and being as quiet as a flame on a candle. Again I saw Ark's head emerge out of the storm cellar like a periscope on a submarine. He turned ever so slowly, looking in every direction, and then his head sunk again. I decided to stay put to see what was going on.

While I sat there, Mama came out the back door, walked around for a minute or two, and then picked a pear, polished it on her apron, sat down on the steps, and ate it. I guess pears don't kill mamas if they eat them at night! As Mama finished her pear, Mrs. Drake came outside, and they met at the border of the yards and talked a bit. When they parted, Mrs. Drake got a watering jug from her porch and soaked the two huge elephant's ear plants that flanked her steps. When they were both gone and my pear consumed, I started down the tree for the second time, only to stop when I saw Ike come out his back door, unfold his Abraham Lincolnesque frame, and sit on the steps.

A short time later, Ark stuck his head out of the storm cellar and sounded a low whistle in Ike's direction, causing him to rise in slow motion. He walked around very casually, stopping to straighten the ferns, picked up a weed to chew on and then, as quick as a turtle, descended into the storm cellar. I saw a hand come up out of the deep, grab the door, and shut it quietly. What were two grown men doing in a dark storm cellar this late in the early darkness? I started down the tree for the third time, again only to freeze in motion when Mrs. Drake came out of the house again and stood like a statue on the porch. I figured she was looking for Ark and Ike, so I went back up to my perch.

After looking around, she walked over toward the storm cellar and acted as if she were listening for something. It was then that she walked deliberately over to the house, picked up a garden hoe, and came back to the storm cellar door. Without saying a word, she lifted the hoe, and for two or three minutes she beat the hell out of that door. I had never before, nor after, seen such a dramatic and violent bit of moral judgment exacted on children by their parent. Mrs. Drake left no one in doubt, especially Ark and Ike, how she felt about the issue. She left, placed the hoe in its place, and went inside.

Later that night, when I was in bed, I heard the rusty hinges of the storm cellar squeak, and then I saw two shadowy figures emerge from underground and go inside.

This village drama comes to mind occasionally, and I get a laugh, now that I know what was in those two jugs; I'm now sure it wasn't water. I still long for another chance to sit in my perch atop the chinaberry tree, above the action, being quiet, with nothing to do but to rest in the stillness and be a boy again.

Splitting Spit

BIG FAMILIES WERE THE NORM in our village. The families with many children were treasured by the mill company. As mentioned earlier, a big family meant many good hands to work. Our family, with nine children, was above average, even though there were larger families around. These were not Catholic families in which birth control was a not-too-effective rhythm method. They were Protestant families whose passions overwhelmed reason. Birth control was regulated by nature. As long as a baby was breastfeeding, pregnancy did not happen, and when the "change of life" occurred, no more babies were going to appear.

Children were everywhere. The schools were full, the streets were overflowing, and swelled stomachs indicated more to come. Children played, and that was their chief occupation, especially in the summer weeks. Where we played was any place in the village big enough to accommodate the game. We had no adult supervision, except when we made too much noise and had to be reminded that some people worked at night: "You boys go someplace else and play; Hershel's got to get his sleep" or "Get the hell out of here and don't come back—you hear me?"

I never remember being bored, but I do recall times in which I could do nothing slowly. Boredom was not part of village life for the kids. There was always something and somewhere to play—not big things, just ordinary things. When I put on a clean pair of overalls on Monday morning, they were expected to last all week. Most of my overalls had patches on the knees from playing marbles on the ground, and I remember one pair that had a small nail pushed through the fabric of the clasp to hold it up because the metal button was missing. Mama had put it there in a hurry one morning, as a quick way to repair them, but she never got around to sewing on a button. After a wash or two that nail rusted, and I was wearing them the day the photographer came to take school pictures. There I sat, with that rusty nail very prominently displayed. My overalls had a little slim, long pocket on the bib for a pencil, and a new penny pencil placed there made me feel quite special.

Overalls were worn by the boys in our school except the bosses' boys, who wore pants and shirts. Azzie boiled my overalls in the big black pot every Monday, scrubbed them on the rub board, put them in starch, and ironed them every week. On Sundays my overalls were on the floor of the dirty-clothes closet, resting for another run. Sunday was a totally different day because all day long we wore our Sunday go-to-meeting clothes, didn't play, and went to church.

There were garages in the back alleys, owned by the mill and rented to those few people who had automobiles. We used the garages for another very quiet activity. With boyhood agility, we climbed to the roofs of those garages as quick as squirrels and lay on our backs watching the slow-moving clouds reconfigure themselves into amazing people, places, and things. "Look over there," someone would say. "That one looks like old Hawkshaw," and we would all laugh. Hawkshaw was our local village policeman, and he eyeballed us like a bird of prey circling over a rabbit burrow. We watched clouds become trees, the number six, a funny-shaped car, and a shapely girl. We were artists painting with our imaginations, until we heard, "Get off my garage—you gonna kill yourself!" yelled by some adult from a back porch. Then we jumped off and ran away. Authority was authority.

Let us find anything out of the ordinary, and we would invent a way to play with it. A few toy balloons were an invitation to an afternoon of excitement: "Let's send them up!" We would scatter to find the necessary and magic materials for the launch. Mama always had a can of Red Devil Lye, and an empty RC Cola bottle was easy to find, but a small piece of aluminum was hard to come by. Very often, if we found an old pot that had been tossed out, we would make a mental note of where it was and go find it when "launching" was to take place. The usual launch site was the big metal manhole cover in my backyard. We would place a small piece of aluminum in the RC Cola bottle, add a spoonful of Red Devil Lye, followed with a few drops of water. That stuff would start boiling and whirling, and a stinking gas would come out the top. That's when we would stretch a balloon over the top, until it was filled with gas, when we'd tie the balloon off with a string. It was ready and raring to hit the sky. All the balloons we had would be filled with that stinking stuff. We had learned this trick from my older brother Edward. He told us that one day there had been a man sitting behind the company store sending balloons. He had been a tall red-haired man they had never seen before. He showed Edward and a couple of other boys how to do it, cautioning them to not try it themselves: "It's very dangerous and can put your eyes out."

We held the balloons until all were ready, and then we wrote notes and attached them, giving the lucky persons who found the balloon our addresses so they would write us and tell how far our balloon had traveled. "One—two—three!" and we would let them all go at the same time.

"I bet mine goes farther than yours."

"I believe mine will go all the way to Piedmont."

"Heck, mine might go to Table Rock."

Our minds were filled with grand schemes, but probably none of them ever got further than the village. We never heard from anybody, but for a few bright, shining moments we played, which was a form of worship, because we had lost ourselves in wonder. We had to leave that RC Cola bottle alone for a while after filling the balloons because it got hot as fire from whatever went on in it to produce that stinking stuff. Later in life, in chemistry lab, we learned that we had made helium in that RC Cola bottle. But at the time it was magic.

There was a dump at the back of the mill, and we were warned, "Don't go around that old dump; you'll get hurt." The dump contained a wonderful assortment of things, tossed there because they were worn out or broken; many had sharp edges. We knew if we could sneak into the dump there would be some amazing thing there that we could use to make some play time. Maybe there would be a worn out "picker stick," which made the best baseball bat in the world. If we were lucky, there would be a spool with some thread still on it, from which we would make a "baseball" by taking a small metal nut and winding the thread real tight, around and around, until it was the size we needed. Then we would find some black tape to wrap around it, so it would not come unraveled in flight.

Word would get out that we had a baseball and a bat, and a crowd would gather. Boys of all ages played. There were two fields in the village large enough to play baseball; one was the schoolyard and the other was beside the mill. All the little boys were placed in the outfield, behind the regular player—they were really ball chasers. A long-hit ball might make it to the tall grass, and a lost ball would end the game, so the little boys had the very important task of watching where the ball landed. When it came time to bat, the little boys would say to one of the big boys, "You bat for me, and I'll run the bases."

Inevitably, one of the bigger boys would hit a ball that would be a homer in Yankee Stadium, and it would land in that darn tall grass. A lost ball suspended action. We would all go to the tall grass, and after a quick search produced no ball, someone would say, "Somebody better *split the spit.*" One of the bigger boys would step to the center of the grass, spit a glob of spit into his palm, and say, "Y'all watch real good." He would hit the spit with the side of his other hand, several globs of spit would fly into the air, and one would land on the lost ball.

If this action did not find the hidden ball after a few tries, we would all go into the tall grass and let spit fly. Soon, "Here it is!" would ring out.

Walking back to resume the game, someone would say, "It'll do it every time." The magic had worked, and the game continued.

That mill dump was our sporting-goods store and the luckiest of boys would find a *steelie* there. A steelie was a ball bearing big enough to use as a toy in a game of marbles. Or maybe we would find four cog wheels about the same size, from which a wagon could be made.

"Don't ever let me hear of you going into that dump or I'll give you a whupping."

We went anyway. It was worth the risk!

I Would Rather Die
Owing You

OLD DOC BATES WAS OUR village druggist, and the drugstore was the best place to buy penny candy. He kept a glassed-in case full of everything from Tootsie Rolls to Guess What? candy, and with a nickel you could buy a little sack full. When I was about twelve years old, I saw on the cigar shelf a tin cigar box that had only three cigars left in it. "Doc, can I have that box when it's empty?"

"Yeah! I will keep it for you."

About a week later I was in the drugstore, and he said, "I gotcha box in the back, if you still want it, Billy."

A metal cigar box with Hav-A-Tampa stamped into the metal top was the best thing in the world to keep your stuff safe. This one had a flip-top lid and would seal completely. I used it as a cash box for my latest enterprise, which was selling candy in the village. I had a small notebook to record my sales—especially those who owed me because they bought "on credit."

A man in an old Chevrolet with a badly broken windshield showed up one morning down at the corner. I passed by him on my way to take a bath at the village bathhouse. The mill owners provided two community bathhouses, one for men and one for women. They were centrally located near the gymnasium. We took our own towels and soap at least once a week for a bath. On that morning, the man in the old Chevrolet spoke to me. "Hey, young man, do you want to make some money?"

That started me off on a new enterprise. I would become the village "candy boy." He gave me two boxes of assorted candy bars, mostly Hershey candy, and said, "You sell them all and bring me back two dollars and forty cents, and I will give you eighty cents—I'll trust you until next week."

I did not go to the bathhouse but went straight home to tell Mama about my new job. She was proud of me. "Did he tell you his name?"

"No, ma'am."

She looked over the two boxes of candy bars. "I'll buy the first one 'cause I love these Mounds bars—I'll give you the nickel on Friday."

I had made my first sale, and even though it was Mama, I recorded the sale "on credit" in my business notebook. That sale made me feel good, but not half as good as having my own metal cigar box.

I kept my stuff in the corner of the drawer where my socks and drawers were. With my new metal box in hand, I went there and transferred my stuff. I had a ball of silver tinsel taken from chewing-gum wrappers, a rock that had some streaks of blue in it, my baseball cards (one mailed to me from Lou Gehrig when I joined the Lou Gehrig Fan Club), an Indian-head penny, one Brazil nut, a shiny bolt that I found in the road (it must have fallen off a real fancy car), and several tobacco tags used to play "puff the tags." It was a boy's treasure chest.

I went from door to door selling Snickers bars, Mr. Goodbars, Milky Ways, Baby Ruths, Mounds, Almond Joys, Hershey bars with almonds, and plain milk-chocolate bars. The easiest place to sell candy seemed to be at the village gymnasium, where boys and men played pickup or "twofers" basketball on the open courts. There was a teenaged boy who had dropped out of school to go to work in the mill who hung around the gymnasium. One day he bought two Mr. Goodbars and told me he would pay me Friday. Several times I asked him for my dime. He always was broke. I kept asking him, and one day he told me that he really did not remember buying any candy from me and to stop asking or he would beat me up. I was learning business the hard way.

I was advised by Mama to not go out to the company store to sell my candy because Mr. Drake, the manager, might not like it. One day, as the company store was closing, I passed by Mr. Drake getting into his car. He said, "Billy, what kind of candy you got to sell?"

"All I got left is two Mounds."

He said, "I'll take them," gave me a quarter, and said something I had never heard before, "Keep the change."

What a nice thing for him to do, especially since he had a store full of candy bars. I told Mama about what Mr. Drake had done. "He's the best manager we ever had at the store," she said.

I kept my candy on top of the Frigidaire and sometimes the money. I trusted my family to leave it alone or if they took a candy bar to put their nickel in the box; seems like some of them forgot to put their nickels in, because when I counted up, I was always a few nickels short.

A man on the paint crew that painted the outside of the village houses in the summer months asked me one day for three Snickers bars on credit. "I'll pay when I get paid." I never saw him again.

"They fired him last week" one of the other painters told me. I was definitely learning the hard way.

For many weeks Mr. No Name came to the exact place, and we did our business. "Boy, you really can sell candy. You want to take three boxes this week?" That would mean more profit—if I could not sell too much "on credit" to folks who didn't pay and if my family would stay out of my candy box. I took the three boxes, which meant I would make a dollar and twenty cents. I decided to keep my candy under my metal cigar box and my money inside the metal box, under my drawers. This plan proved to be a good one.

There were two Mounds bars in each box every week, and I always took one out to give to Mama and I gave another one away each week. In the big house next to the company store lived a family who had a girl, Dorothy, who did not go to school; she was about my age. She stayed inside the backyard fence most of the time, just looking, smiling, and waving at people as they passed by. Early in my candy business days, I passed her standing at the fence, and she waved. I walked over and gave her a Mounds bar. She took it and sat on her back porch steps and ate it. I made sure, each week, to go by and give Dorothy her Mounds. The barber always bought two Mr. Goodbars. The man next door always bought two Snickers. I had regular customers, and it was an easy job and fun. I soon became known as the "village candy man."

The young man who played the organ at the Methodist Church in the village ate his lunch at the café, and I knew he was always going to buy candy from me. "Billy, I left my money over at the church. Come with me to get it," he'd say.

But in my mind I heard something Mama had told me some time before: "Don't go fooling around with that man at the church, 'cause he's 'quaire.'" I did not know what she meant, but I did not go with him. I was afraid.

My best customer was the star of the village baseball team, the Dunean Dynamos. "Ap" Powell was a big redhead who could knock the ball far over the fence in centerfield—a huge, laughing, fun-loving man. He was the best first baseman I had ever seen. Ap dated my sister Louise a few times, and we all liked him. He loved Milky Ways, and one night he bought three of them and said, "Here's one for you, Billy. I'll pay you when I get paid on Friday—that okay?"

He did not pay me that Friday or the next one, and I only asked him once. I disliked asking people who owed me for my money. He said, "Billy, I would rather die owing you than to beat you out of it." I never did get my fifteen cents. Ap went on to play professional baseball in the Washington Senators organization. He still owed me fifteen cents when he died years later, and I remembered he'd said, "I'd rather die than beat you out of it."

One day I kept watching for the man in the car with the badly broken windshield, but he never came. I owed him for two boxes of candy, a dollar and sixty cents. He never came back, and I was out of business. I put his money and mine in my cigar box. About a week later, I found that someone had taken a dollar from my tin box (and I know who took it). I got so mad I went under the house and with the hoe dug a hole and buried my box with everything in it. About that time, my mind went on to other things, probably girls or another enterprise, and I forgot about that box in the dirt under the house.

I guess until this day that box is still there, with my Lou Gehrig card, my ball of tinfoil, and all of a boy's treasures.

The "Ob" Legacy

OLIVER WAS BIGGER THAN ALL of us. He had failed two grades before he got to the sixth grade. He was a gentle boy, but Oliver was dull. He never seemed to have pencil or paper and did not do his homework. He was called "Ob," an appropriate-sounding name for the oaf-like boy he was. OB were the initials for Oliver Bell. I liked Ob because he made us laugh, mostly at himself. He said odd things in class, like, "Miss Foster, do you ever wonder why the sky is blue?" We all knew the answer: God wanted it blue! One day Ob asked Miss Foster, a truly gifted generator and producer of the "teachable moment," this: "My Mama said butterflies can make cloth. Is that right?"

Cloth was the ultimate end product of all the energy expended by the village folks. Fiber came from the cotton fields, and after dozens of processes, finished cloth was ready for shipment to clothing manufacturers. For someone to suggest that cloth was made by a butterfly was just as absurd as another of his questions, "Miss Foster, if you had wings, could you fly?"

In the human endeavor to learn, there are three factors that, if used in harmony, can make life "sing and zing." These three basically nonmeasurable quotients compose the mental work of all people. The first is IQ, the intelligence quotient, and its subsequent development into intellect. The second is SQ, the social quotient, the elemental process that determines how we relate to all living matter in our world (or basically how we get along with other people and life). Without SQ and its development, IQ is sterile, meaningless, and nonserviceable. The third quotient is CQ. The curiosity quotient, the third component in this triad, is human evolution's grand gift to us. This factor is best manifested in human imagination. CQ is the locus where life sparkles and shines, the mental playground where restraint and restriction are not present. Without a modicum of CQ, life never takes flight or soars above the rooftops of routine, and we become grounded in the mundane.

Ob might have lacked the IQ and SQ essential to making school successful, but he had CQ in abundance. I do not know what his life was like after he left school, but I would bet he created an interesting world around him.

"Miss Foster, do butterflies make cloth?"

An alert professional teacher can sense when the time is ripe to apply all the professional dexterity and skill necessary to cause learning to occur. Miss Foster hopped to the center of our lives and caused learning to explode in that sixth-grade class in our village school. She certainly knew the answer and could have shown her knowledge on the subject by some lecture, but she did not do it. Instead she "massaged" the idea into very meaningful curriculum.

Over the next weeks we experienced the cycle of life in our classroom. Miss Foster secured a huge aquarium and a bunch of green mulberry leaves covered with tiny black silkworm eggs smaller than poppy seeds. She placed several twigs in the aquarium along with the mulberry leaves and silkworm eggs. Where did she get them? How do teachers know where to find all they need to create a lesson? Could it be they have a secret place just for those who have highly curious students?

Those tiny black eggs soon hatched into small green worms, which ate the mulberry leaves and grew fat as garden caterpillars. They ate so heartily that we had to find more mulberry leaves for their food. All during this process, we were reading about the making of silk in China, even learning about the great Silk Road, which led us into the history of silk trade. We were asked to bring in scraps of silk from home for an exhibit. Mama let me take a silk handkerchief that my Papa had worn in his coat pocket.

In the aquarium, those worms, which looked like tiny Chinese dragons, crawled all over the twigs, going about doing whatever silkworms do. Of all the tiny black eggs, only a dozen hatched and lived to maturity. After we had watched the silkworm show for several weeks, they all attached themselves to twigs and proceeded to wrap their bodies in very thin golden thread, which came from their rear ends. Soon they were totally wrapped—we learned they were called cocoons. We read about what was happening inside the cocoons and learned a new word, *larvae*. If all went right, and it did, the worms would change into butterflies. Miss Foster said they were really called moths. We divided the cocoons into two groups. One group was used to harvest the silk threads, and the others were allowed to burst open and the butterfly take flight. This was the feature activity I recall from sixth grade—we learned so much!

One day Dr. Hollis, the superintendent of schools, visited our class to see the project he had heard about from our school principal. He bragged on us, and we gave him one of the cocoons to take with him. Many years later I found out that all the sixth grades in the school system from that time on had a silkworm science project as a part of their curriculum.

Ob, the boy with the elevated curiosity quotient, never got the answer to his question, because he dropped out of school and went to work at a dairy farm before the silkworm project had progressed very far. The boy took flight but, unknown to him, he left a legacy—a legacy born from his overactive and highly elevated curiosity.

The Movies

IT NEVER RAINED ON SATURDAYS. The sun was always warm, and we were free as running water. Nobody called me up saying, "Time to get ready for school" or "Time for church." It was Saturday, and all the clocks stopped. The sun woke me up, I put on the shirt and short pants I had worn yesterday, went to the kitchen, poured a cup of coffee, added the biscuit, sugar and milk, and proceeded to eat my coffee with a spoon.

Mama's throne was on the front porch. It was a rocking chair where she read the morning paper, peeled potatoes, and spoke to all the villagers who passed by on their way to places unknown. On Saturdays she always had a few coins in her apron pocket because Saturday was allowance day.

Saturdays were created to give boys a break from school and to allow us to have a fun day before the next day, which had only one redeeming quality—fried chicken for lunch. The long, long wait at church was tolerable only because of the promise of fried chicken once we were finally free from the long-windedness of the preacher.

"Y'all going to the movie today?"

Did she have to ask? Saturday was movie day. My front porch was the gathering spot from which all things wonderful were launched. From all directions in the village they came, that inseparable bunch: Lard Mason, Stein Granger, Wadd Meadows, R. W. Donnan, Wayne Davis, and me, Billy Hale.

"Y'all will have to walk today; I don't have enough money for carfare," Mama said as she reached into her apron pocket and gave me a dime and a nickel. Fifteen cents was just enough for a movie ticket and a box of popcorn.

By midmorning we were all ready to go. We walked past the drugstore, company store, barbershop, and mill office, around back of the mill, and by the mill pond to get on the railroad track, which would lead us "uptown." We wore no shoes, as our feet were toughened from experience. From my house to the Rivoli Theater, using the trolley, was three miles, but if we walked the railroad cut it was only two miles. Our route took us past an old honky tonk. "Don't y'all even look in that direction," Mama warned.

The railroad took us over a high trestle, which was scary to cross, because we could look down into a deep ravine and creek bed between the crossties. After that, we had to walk beside the huge cotton warehouse, where it was believed that a tribe of gypsies lived among the bales of cotton, coming out at night to build a fire and cook beside the railroad track. Invariably, when we passed that warehouse someone in our gang would swear they saw one of the gypsy girls looking out the window at us, and we would all run for our lives.

For about half a mile we had to walk through the village where the black people lived. We were told to never stop there for any reason: "Don't look to the right or left, and keep on walking as fast as you can." As we neared town, we passed Claussen's Bakery, which emitted an aroma that created visions of fresh-baked loaves of bread and cakes from big ovens. After walking for forty minutes, we came to the River Bridge at the lower end of Main Street. The Rivoli Theater was at the upper end of the street.

The Rivoli was the "cowboy" movie house. We would watch the Pathé newsreel, a cartoon, a comedy, and if we were lucky, it would be the *Three Stooges* and then the next episode of the "continued." "Continueds" were serials, with fifteen episodes of *Buck Rogers*, *Flash Gordon*, or *Men from Mars*. At the end of each week's episode the hero would be in some unbelievable peril, but in the next week's episode he would have miraculously survived only to find himself in a similar predicament. Then we would see the cowboy feature of the week, hoping it was not one of those singing cowboys.

Our boxes of popcorn were the treat of the week. We tried to get the popcorn man to leave the tops open so he could put more in the boxes. Every week we made a contest out of eating the popcorn. How much could we eat without touching it, simply by biting it out of the top of the box? We made a lot of noise doing that. All of us sat there looking like horses with feed bags. We never knew the time when the movie began. We went in and stayed until it started over, often staying for a second showing.

Stein had a special and peculiar talent, which he had developed to perfection. He could make the sound of a huge fart by squeezing his hands together. Inevitably, at the precise moment when the cowboy kissed his girlfriend or his horse at the end of the movie, Stein would let it rip! We would laugh, say "Shoo-wee," and leave the area where he was sitting, acting as if he stunk.

Heading back home we frantically acted out anything we had seen in the movie, especially if we had seen the *Three Stooges*, which gave us ideas about making sounds when we hit each other. We were total fools, free as the wind, with no restraints. Stein would walk stiffly, like a monster; I would jump on Wadd's back and ride him like a cowboy, while R. W. and Lard would walked ahead of us, saying, "We don't know them—they are from *Pelzer.*" All this took place on Main Street, where many people were shopping and gazing at us as if we had escaped the crazy house.

We got back on the railroad leading to the village and entertained ourselves by seeing who could walk the longest distance balancing on one rail, or by all of us standing on one crosstie and seeing who could pee the farthest. Golden streams arched in an Olympic pissing contest.

Our Saturday movie excursion consumed the day, five or six hours totally unsupervised and free of worry. We were boys being boys, and being boys was our chief occupation.

The route back to the village took us past the mill pond. No self-respecting boy could pass by that pond without tossing a rock over the fence to try to disturb Old Ben, the most amazing fish ever to live—but that is another story. We were ready now to face the rigors of the next day, when we would not be free to be boys.

The Strange Tale of Goings McDouwitt or "Hey, Mister! What's in That Little Bag?"

OUR VILLAGE WAS CALM, COMPACT, and commonplace. We were the source of our own excitement most of the time. Our highest dramas were snowstorms or a wreck on the highway. Occasionally an outside source would raise the excitement level, such things as the annual visit of the professional basketball team, The House of David, which featured the world's greatest long-shot artist, Little Davy Banks. He dazzled us with his talent; he had previously played with the original New York Celtics. A flutter might also be caused by a new family moving to our village with a house full of pretty girls. In the summer of 1936, the excitement level had stagnated. All our days were common, routine, and "same-same," until—!

He came into our lives like Halley's Comet, creating a summer of unusual and unforgettable drama. Like a comet, glowing brightly and then fading deep into the blue of time and space, Goings McDouwitt came and went as quickly as the flame on a matchstick, but leaving years of conversation in the afterglow. None of us would ever forget that summer! Goings McDouwitt was as strange as his name, a different kind of man—if he was a man! He was taller than most tall men, topped with bright, kinky hair as red as cherries on a banana split, and as slim as a cornstalk. He wore black knickers, black stockings, and green shoes with a huge silver buckle on each one. His sweater-shirt was dark green, with one sleeve much shorter than the other one. Goings McDouwitt was his real name; McDouwitt was pronounced, "Mac-do-it."

Goings had been born in Dublin, Ireland, in the centennial year of 1900. His father had been a Catholic priest who fell in love with a very young girl whose family served as the sextons in the school where he taught. An affair followed, and much to their surprise, their family started before their marriage. This caused them great problems, and he had to leave the school. Sean Lochland McDouwitt and Erin O'Looney lived in Dublin for a half dozen years after the baby was born. Sean continued to teach but in one of the city schools. It was during these very difficult years that Goings became an avid reader. His father, known as Father Mac, had brought his library with him when he left the Catholic school, and it contained many of the classics. The tales about gypsies attracted Goings very much. He also loved the books about the Norwegian gods and gnomes.

Life in Ireland became so stressful because of their fight for freedom from the British crown that the McDouwitts fled to Amsterdam, Holland. After being there only a year, Goings's parents died in the of the great flu epidemic, leaving him orphaned. He was placed in an orphanage workhouse at the age of thirteen. He ran away from the workhouse and stowed away on a cargo ship. At sea he was discovered and forced to work as a sailor. He fell in love with ocean life, serving on that same ship for several years. The captain of the ship was a kind man who had a well-stocked bookshelf, and he encouraged Goings to read his books.

Once Goings nearly lost his life in a massive storm; the ship lost its mainsail and had to limp into port. They anchored in the harbor at Charleston, South Carolina. Goings never went back to sea. He found a bookstore in town, called Stacks, and he became a clerk there. The people who traded at Stacks were fascinated by this tall redhead who whistled beautifully as he worked around the books and who told amazing stories from his early days in Ireland. He attracted much attention at this bookstore. He was unusual, dressed theatrically, became a storyteller for young people, and whistled constantly. He was mysterious. No one ever saw Goings anyplace except at work or on the bench at the park. They never saw him come or go and did not know where he lived. They never saw him on the street or in church. His lunchtime most days was spent at a nearby park, where he whittled, whistling all the while. People found it difficult to walk by him when they saw his whittling and heard him whistling.

Except for the time he and his parents lived in Amsterdam, Goings had missed the opportunity to go to school. However, as a boy he had developed a love for books and reading. This had been intensified while he was at sea. Even though he was young, his fellow sailors cherished his telling of the stories he had learned from his dad, "Father Mac." At his father's side he had heard great stories of mystery and the forces of nature, especially the "spirit of the wind." He and his father had often sat in the grass beside a huge windmill near their home, and Goings had heard stories about the "voices" of the wind, stories decorated well with the actual sounds of the wind. Each of these stories had ended with the same eight-note tune performed by Father Mac's brilliant whistling. Goings soon began to call it "the wind-singing song."

While Goings went ashore from sea, he always tried to find bookstores, even though his sea mates sought rum and women. He traded his small carvings for the books. These were carvings of small animals from a special wood from Africa.

When Goings was a small boy of eight, he'd spent a summer in Shannon, Ireland, on the opposite coast from Dublin, with his mother's parents. His grandparents were Gaither and Gayla O'Looney. They were fun-loving people who worked hard in their home craft of furniture making. Their tables and cabinets were treasured by anyone who bought them because of their extraordinary quality. One of their features was hand-carved flowerets attached to the furniture as decoration. Gaither was an exquisite whittler, and he loved to whittle small crosses, which he gave to all the children of his village.

Gaither had been born in Limerick, just twenty miles inland from Shannon, into a family of wood craftsmen. The O'Looney clan had a ritual of long standing. When a boy turned eight years old, they held a ceremony at which he was given his own carving knife with sharp blades and tools. It was a rite of passage. He could now join the men as they sat around the fire in the long winter evenings, whittling and whistling. Gaither demonstrated exceptional talent, producing exciting designs the others had never seen. Soon he was carving walking canes with greatly detailed figures and vines that curved around the stick. Word spread of his beautiful canes: "If you can find a Gaither cane, it is worth a fortune."

The O'Looney family were fine whittlers but equally well known for their amazing talent as whistlers. Their tones were clear and flute-like in quality. It was not unusual for villagers to come and stand around their house to listen when they were whittling and whistling. They whistled in harmony and knew all the favorite folk songs.

While Goings was visiting the O'Looneys that summer, they conducted the knife ceremony for him. He received his blade for carving and soon joined the men as they whittled and whistled. He quickly learned both art forms. "Gayla, come hear Goings whistle," Gaither said. "He's got the prettiest tone of all of us. He is really good."

On the day before Goings was to return to Dublin from this summer trip, his grandfather took him out to the family wood house and gave him two small leather drawstring bags. "Here is a bag to carry your blades and some wood for carving, and in this small bag is a special gift I want you to have."

"What is it, Grandpa?"

Gaither opened the bag and held a carving in his palm. "It is very special, and it will bring you a world full of wonder."

"What do you call it?"

"It's a *bunga ball*, and the wood came from Africa. An old gypsy who came through here many years ago traded some dark wood for one of my walking canes."

"Can I hold it?"

Gaither gave him the carving. Goings knew he held the most fascinating carving he had ever seen. It was a circular piece of very dark wood about the size of a big apple. It had five ribs, making a cage for a small wooden ball of the same wood inside the cage. "It feels warm! Did you carve this?"

"Yes! I did it as a gift for my mother, and when she died I put it in this bag. Now I want you to have it."

"For keeps?"

"Sure, it is yours forever. My mother loved it and told me it contained the spirit of the wind."

The piece of wood the old gypsy had given to Gaither O'Looney in exchange for one of his fancy walking canes was bunga wood, which grows in South Africa and is used by artists all over the world to carve small objects such as rabbits and swans. These art pieces are coveted by people for their beautiful artistic value—we have a small bunga-wood carving of a pelican in our dining room.

After about five years working as a clerk in the bookstore in Charleston, Goings grew restless and began to hear the "spirit of the wind" calling him toward the mountains of South Carolina. He had enjoyed Charleston and working at Stacks Bookstore, and he had made enough money to buy a car. He bought a black Model A Ford, which had only one front seat but a big trunk area. It was an unusual car. He kept it shining like a little girl's black patent-leather shoes. Packing his book collection and the two leather drawstring bags containing the prized bunga ball and his whittling tools, Goings headed toward the mountainous area to seek another bookstore for employment and to be near the spirit of the wind, which he found more readily in the mountains.

Back in those days and nights sitting around the fire with grandfather Gaither in Limerick, Goings had heard well-crafted stories, stories that could charm a sleeping cat to wake up and listen, stories that captivated young and old alike. Gaither's stories flowed with excitement and mystery and always had a surprise punch line. Goings learned this craft from the master. He had become the most entertaining storyteller in the coastal area of South Carolina, scheduling regular "story hours" for children, but he soon found that people of all ages came to hear his amazing yarns. It helped that his appearance was unusual, that he had a heavy Irish accent, a smile as big as a Cheshire cat's, cherry-red hair, and deep-blue Irish eyes. He had the habit of holding the bunga ball in his hand while telling a story; he fondled it as he talked but never referred to it. He made it rattle occasionally. All this made him magnetically attractive.

It was in the late summer of 1936 that Goings first came to our village. No one knew why he came. He was simply there. The men at the village barbershop said that one morning he parked his car in front of the shop and sat in the car for a long time, just looking around, whistling some tune over and over. They said his whistling was bright and loud, like a flute. After sitting there awhile, he got out of the shiny Model A, took a small leather bag from the trunk, and came into the shop for a trim. He said only, "Can I get a cut?"

Goings held the leather bag while he was in the chair. When Mr. Cartee, the shop owner, finished his hair, Goings left, saying, "Good day to ye, kind sirs." They stood at the window and watched him drive off—it was a strange sight.

Word of the strange man at the barbershop traveled through the village like a summer thunderstorm. Two weeks later we heard that the strange redheaded man was sitting on the front steps of the Methodist church, whittling and whistling.

"Don't get too close to that man, no telling what he's up to," Mama said when I told her the strange man was back and I was going to see him.

As I walked toward the church, about a dozen kids were converging on the church from all directions. The news of the strange man's presence had traveled quickly that morning. We passed a black man, Rob, whose job was to walk the streets of the village picking up trash. He said, "The barber says it's the same man that was here before."

We walked cautiously to where he sat. The first thing I noticed was his cherry-red hair, very neatly combed, and his pursed lips, from which came flute-like sounds that penetrated the air all around. We edged closer and sat down. There was a constant smile on his face, which gave me the same feeling I got when my Uncle Batson came to visit us. He always brought a feeling of security and sense that nothing could go wrong as long as he was there. The sun was bright that July morning. The tall oak trees caused dappled shadows that moved like a ballet on the grass where we had started to sit down. Goings sat whittling and whistling but never looked up. There was a long extended silence. Finally, he looked up. He said nothing, just smiled.

One of the Lollis girls asked, "Where you from, mister?"

With a twinkle in his eyes, he pointed to his black, shiny car and said, "I'm from wherever my car came from today." He laughed. "No! I came from the last place." He laughed again.

He kept on whittling and whistling. I asked, "What kind of wood is that you are cutting on?" It was a very black wood, and I had never seen black wood before.

"This is bunga wood, from Africa."

"Can I have one of the pieces you cut off?"

"You can have a whole piece, if you want it." Reaching into his bag, he pulled out a handful of pieces the size of dominoes. "All of you can have one if you would like."

He stood. My, my! He was so tall. He gave each of us a piece of bunga wood. "If you hold it tight, it will touch you back."

I squeezed mine; it felt alive and moving. Goings went back to whittling and whistling.

"What's in that little bag?" Frances asked him.

"What's your name?"

"Frances! What's your name?"

"Goings McDouwitt."

Time did not move quickly that morning. Everything seemed slowed down. After a few moments, McDouwitt picked up the small leather drawstring bag and told us the story of his grandfather's carving ability and how he came to have the most extraordinary special carving that he had ever seen. He held the small bag up and asked, "Do you want to see it?"

We all said, "Yes!"

About that time, Lard stood up and said, "Hey, Mr. McGoings."

Goings did not correct him.

"This piece of wood is moving in my hand."

"Mine too!" came from half a dozen voices.

"Oh, it's just saying hello," Goings said.

When he finally took the carving out of the bag, he held it up high in his palm and said, "This is a bunga ball." It was beautiful black wood, like the small pieces he had given us. He passed it around, and as we took turns holding it, he whistled. You could see through it and see the small ball inside the cage. When he got it back, he held it up again, and we all got quiet. He began to whistle a short tune over and over. Then he stopped suddenly and said, "It has the spirit of the wind."

Frances asked, "What'chu mean, the 'spirit of the wind'? Is it hainted?"

Goings told a story, and as he told the story, time seemed to stop passing. "While I was sailing off the coast of India a few years ago, a massive storm tossed our ship around so badly it broke the mainmast and we had to limp into port. The storm lasted several days. One evening during the great typhoon, I went out on deck. I had this bunga ball with me. When I held it up to the wind, the little ball inside began to float, and the wind going through the bunga ball whistled the tune my grandfather used to whistle back in Ireland." Goings then whistled the tune, holding the bunga ball high in the air. It reminded me of a hymn we sang in church. It was a soothing sound that made me feel as if a storm had just passed and soft breezes had replaced the fierce blasts.

He ended the story, and we all sat quietly while he whittled and whistled. Suddenly he stopped and looked around at all the black shavings lying on the steps and grass. He said, "Oh, me! I've made a mess."

He put the bunga ball back in the bag, secured all his tools and the unfinished carving, and said, "Gotta be going." The tall redheaded Irishman stood, and on his way to his car he gave each of us a gentle pat on the head, saying, "*Sheee!*" which is the Gaelic word for "peace." Goings McDouwitt got in his shiny black car and drove off, never looking back.

We watched him descend the long highway leading away from the village. The car turned the slow curve at the bottom of the hill and disappeared. Goings was gone! It was a summer we would always remember. It was a summer when, for a few bright shining moments, we were enchanted by an event with dreamlike quality.

We all scattered because it was dinnertime back at our houses. When I got home, Mama was sitting on the front porch reading the *Saturday Evening Post* while waiting for the cornbread to finish baking. I told her about the strange man at the Methodist church, about his bunga ball, and told her that he had given each of us a small piece of bunga wood. I reached into my pocket to show her my piece of wood—and it was gone!

"I thought you had just made up that yarn," Mama said laughingly.

"No, Mama. He was really there—the redheaded man they been talking about—he was there!"

"Billy, you know you just joking with me—don't you?"

I ran as fast as I could back to the church to get a piece of the shavings to prove to Mama what I had seen. When I got there, I did not see shavings on the ground, not even a tiny piece. Where had they all gone?

On the way home I saw Frances, who shouted, "I lost my piece of bunga wood!"

"Me too!"

Within ten minutes, the whole gang who had been at the church discovered that none of us had our bunga wood. We were in total disbelief—even more so when we all went to the church steps to try to find the chips of bunga wood on the ground. There were none there. I asked Frances to go with me to my house to tell Mama I had not made the story up in my own head.

The mystery of the tall redheaded man's visit spread like dandelion seeds in a brisk breeze across the village. Later that day, many folks gathered at the front of the barbershop. There was a buzz in the air. The barbers confirmed they had seen the strange man with bright-red hair and odd clothes sitting on the church steps whittling and whistling. They said he'd had two leather bags in his hand. Frances and I told them of the bunga ball, the pieces of wood he'd given us, and how they had all disappeared. We described how he'd whistled like a flute, how he'd whittled, and how he'd talked about the spirit of the wind. The Baptist preacher who was in the crowd opined, "Sounds like the old devil has gotten in these children, if you ask me." No one had asked him. We knew he was wrong. He continued, "What did that 'bunger' thing look like, Billy?"

"Well, it was about the size of a baseball and carved from black wood. It was a cage that had a small ball about the size of a marble inside the cage, and Goings said it floated when the wind blew, and when you touched it—it touched back. The bunga ball was smooth and looked like furniture."

"Sounds evil to me," the preacher said.

When you are ten years old and it is summertime, the world is magical, mysterious, and filled with curiosity. It is a time when imagination tops reality. When you get older, much older, you can revisit those incredible days and perhaps write a story with childlike wonder.

I do wonder where Goings McDouwitt went on that sun-filled July morning when I was ten years old, when he left our village in his very shiny black Model A Ford, with his two leather bags in the truck. Where did he wander? Where did the unbelievable, magnificent bunga ball go next? I just know he went out of sight around the curve. Was it to another village and some other boy's imagination?

CHURCH

A Frightened Little Boy

CHILDHOOD SHOULD BE A HAPPY-GO-LUCKY, carefree time of life. A young boy ought to be unburdened by the issues in the family. He should never spend school time worrying about something going on in the family that doesn't concern him. A boy ought to fly his mental kites and ride his imaginary carousel and not have his mind fixated on whether or not a storm might come that night. Also, it is tragic when a boy sits on the front-porch swing after school, staring coldly and pondering what the preacher said yesterday about going to hell if you were a sinner, while all the other boys and girls are gleefully playing dodge ball.

If boyhood should be a happy-go-lucky time, I missed a lot of it. I grew up in a big family, with a Mama who took care of my needs and a Papa who was bigger than life, fun-filled, overtly loving, and important in the village. We were an upper lower-class family, based on our finances and lifestyle.

Life was centered on Fridays, which was payday at the mill. Pay envelopes were distributed in the mill at your work site. For a few hours we had money, but that condition wore off by Tuesday. Our family, like most families, "made it" by charging groceries at the company store. For the weekend, we had a bit to spare, enough to go uptown to a movie or to a Saturday-afternoon baseball game. Fridays and Saturdays were good days, but then on Sundays we put on our Sunday-go-to-meeting clothes and went to church. Papa and my brother Ed went to the Methodist church. Mama and the rest of us went to the Baptist church.

My boyhood days would have been far more peaceful and free, spent just being a boy, except for two things: *storms* and *church*.

You learn most by observing, even when you are not conscious of it. Storms scared the shit out of me—I mean literally! I would very often get so frightened my bowels would become loose. I did not come forth from the womb scared of storms. So what drove me to the point of mental illness about the elements?

I blame it on my oldest sister, Emma. She was unusually frightened by lightning and thunder or any other strange behavior of the weather. Emma and Will Vickery lived in the same village where we lived. Anytime of the night, if she heard thunder, she would bring her whole family to our house. I guess she felt secure there. She was a basket case—moaning and groaning as the storm came closer. Seeing her so emotionally distressed and weakened with fear was enough to imprint on me great consternation and confusion about storms. Normally she was a self-assertive, fun-loving, and in-charge person. Why did the storms have such power to reduce her to this irrational, disruptive behavior?

When the wind blew fiercely, you could feel the house creak. It sat on several brick pillars and had no underpinning. I was afraid the house would blow away with us in it. Weather was mysterious, and the only forecast was in the daily paper: "Showers Today" or "Clear and 85." My sister's fear was that any storm could be a tornado. Reports of tornadoes must have contributed to her fright. I realize she must have learned this; she did not come with storm fear as original equipment! Somehow someone had reacted to storms with sheer terror and she had caught it from them like a disease, just as I had caught it from her. Many nights we would already be bedded down for the night when there would be a knock at the door and then the familiar words, "Emmer and 'em are here." We would get up and rearrange our sleeping places, making a big pallet for five or six of us kids to wait out the storm, which she had predicted by lightning far off in the distance. Sometimes the storm came, sometimes not.

From these highly emotional displays by Emma, I became abnormally afraid of storms. When I was seven or eight, I watched the sky with a third eye. I would be playing with the other kids on the block and suddenly see a big cloud or lightning off in the distance. I would stop playing, run home as quickly as I could, and sit on the front porch with Mama, asking her if she thought it was going to be a bad one. More than likely Mama's answer would be dismissive about it, with her saying, "Oh, Billy! I think this one is going down the river." That was of some comfort to me, even though at that moment I remember thinking, "What river?" We lived many miles from a river.

If it snowed too long, I became afraid it would cover the house and we would all die. If it turned too cold, I was afraid it would never get warm again. Once when the wind howled fiercely, for some stupid reason, I went and raised a window and shouted "Help, help!" into the wind. I was crazy with fear of storms.

If your total psychic being is vulnerable to what the weather is going to do, your life is out of balance. During those horrible years of my life no one in the family ever talked to me about storms, or if they did, it was ineffectual. The threat of storms possessed me, and I was a very frightened little boy.

Now, combine all this with the effects the church was having on my mental space every Sunday. I was a basket case! We dressed up and went to church twice on Sundays and back on Wednesday nights for prayer meeting, for which we met in a room downstairs for a midweek dose of hellfire and damnation. The preacher was A. Howard Wilson, a big, rotund man with little hair and a demanding countenance. He preached loud and long with emotion and fiery words—almost always in threatening tones. He was sincere, I suppose. The man kept our sins right out in front of us constantly. It seemed that anything that was fun or had pleasure in it was sin. Don't smoke, chew, gamble, drink bad stuff, cuss, go to "them hellhole movies" or ball games, or have sex in any thought, word, or deed. "Hell awaits you—hell seven times hotter than fire," which I always assumed burned real bad, but never burned you up, but you hurt forever. The devil presided there, yelling and moaning was constant, and you never slept. If you did not get saved and become a baptized person, you would go to hell, and your mama and papa could not help you at all. Now, about "them hellhole movies"—you surely did not want to be sitting in one of them eating your popcorn and watching Buck Jones or Roy Rogers, when the Lord came back. That would be the worst of situations.

Twice a year the church held two-week-long revivals, and you had to go unless you were "providentially hindered," which was an excuse I never got to use because I did not know what it meant. The revivalists were traveling evangelists whose prime role in life was to get you saved and put on the right road to heaven. Heaven was a place where there were no storms (that made it appealing to me), no sickness or pain, and everybody had a house or a palace, which was filled most of the time with people singing hymns and smiling. You did not have to work; all your needs would be taken care of by the angels (except winnie soup, I betcha).

Dying was the worst thing to think about, because if you happened to "not be right with the Lord" at the time—a bit backslid—to hell you went. You never knew for sure whether you had it right. In any event, you had to go before St. Peter at the gate and confess to everything you ever did that was wrong. St. Peter put that on a scale to see whether you got in. Heck, they already knew everything you had done beforehand because it was written in The Book of Life. They just wanted to test your memory. But rest assured, there was no way you could sneak past the gatekeeper.

The evangelist always spent the first night giving his personal testimony about how he had been a sorry, no-good reprobate, out drinking and gambling, and then one night his buddy had invited him to go to a revival meeting to hear the great Brother Isaac Edwards from Dallas, Texas, preach his mighty sermon entitled "There Will Come a Day, My Friend." And then he told how the Holy Spirit had grabbed his heart and propelled him to the front to accept Jesus as his personal savior. That's when he gave up his good job selling cars, gave up drinking and gambling, and started evangelizing.

The second night was always about the "unpardonable sin." The evangelist got really worked up about this one. He yelled and shouted about "blaspheming the Holy Spirit." We did not know what that meant, but his emotion-laden stories were so obscure and obtuse that they left all of us wondering whether we were guilty and headed straight to hell. Taking the Lord's name in vain was part of it, like saying those two biggies together, "Goddamn"—and there I sat remembering that I had said them, or breathed them, a couple of times when I was mad. Woe was me!

On the last Friday night of the two-week revival, the topic was announced as The Second Coming, and I anticipated it with horror and dread. This one was designed to get the last sorry sinner to come down the aisle and "make it right" with the Lord. The message had as its center post the proposition that "in the twinkling of an eye" the trumpet will sound and the rapture will begin. The evangelist spent a lot of time proving that all the signs were in place for Jesus to come back, pointing out that the Antichrist was already here, lurking in the background waiting to make his move, or maybe that the Antichrist was either Hitler or the pope.

His descriptions of this event would leave me trembling and scared out of my mind. I would worry about it for weeks on end. I slowly got over it—and then it would be time for revival again. All this was a massive snow job, but I did not know it then. I had been blindsided by ignorance spoken with authority!

In the early summer of 1933, Papa was operated on for stomach cancer, but the cancer had spread too much and he was at home in bed for months. The older children knew he was dying, but the younger ones, including me, did not know. So when he died it was a shock—a life-altering shock. I was seven years old and in the second grade—and Papa was gone! Mama was a very stoic person and bred her stoicism into us. I never saw my Mama grieve my Papa's death. She sat by the fire with the poker in her hand stirring the ashes night after night and never shed a tear. There was never any talk of Papa's death. We just sucked it up into some deep place and rode out this worst of storms. I did wonder about Papa and whether he was in heaven. I dreamed many times that Papa was still at home, only to waken to the agony again that he was still gone.

When aunts and uncles came to see us, I heard them say of me, "He is the spitting image of his daddy." This made me proud at the time, but this type of thing would come back to haunt me. I did not handle my Papa's death very well. Many of my moments were filled with thoughts about my friends whose daddies were still alive and how I envied them.

My friend and exciting pulpiteer John Claypool said once in a sermon, "If you don't deal with grief creatively, it will deal with you destructively every time." About two years after Papa's death I had become a pitiful little boy who'd experienced many months of hallucinations—bad ones! I saw things big and heard things loud. When the house quieted down at night, things happened. The clock on the fireboard would suddenly enlarge to the size of a basketball and the tick-tock would be like thunder. Or if I was in the kitchen, the table would appear to be moving around and around. These episodes would last for several minutes. The dread of it occurring again kept me in turmoil. The smallest sound would suddenly amplify into a thunderous roar, or things I focused on would begin to come at me, getting bigger and bigger until I flinched and looked at something else.

Death anxiety was very present in my life. Many, many nights when everybody was asleep in my house I would creep quietly to Mama's bed and whisper, "Mama, are you asleep?"

She would respond wisely and kindly, "No, Billy, I'm just resting my eyes." They had said Papa had gone to sleep, a way to avoid using the word *died*. So several times a night I would go check to see if Mama had "gone to sleep."

I was so addled by life that I was unable to live free of the massive worry about things—storms, religion, and death. In the fifth grade I sat with a cold stare, worrying about all these things. As I did not do my school work, they retained me in the fifth grade. I was a failure!

Time is the great healer, and maturity is the change agent. I do not remember and am unable to determine when I began to come out of the stupor that possessed me. Frederick Beuchner wrote, "Sometimes when a leaf falls from the branch and lands in the water of a stream it floats well until it comes to the swirling current of the rocky shoal and is sucked down, only to become silt. However, there are some leaves that, for some reason, call it dumb luck or providence, ride out the turbulence into the placid, peaceful waters beyond the shoals." I was one of those lucky ones—I rode it out.

Other things began to take the place of the life of dread. Perhaps it was the bright, shining gold trumpet my brother George bought for me so I could play in the elementary school band. Maybe it was the music of the big bands who came to the Carolina Theater so my brother and I could go and hear them (sometimes three shows in the same afternoon!). Tommy Dorsey, Glenn Miller, Jack Teagarden, Clyde McCoy, Ina Ray Hutton, and a dozen more big bands brought major change. Perhaps it was a nascent push to put religion in perspective and to honor my own private doubts about that stuff. Perhaps it was going to camp and witnessing that the other boys were not scared out of their minds when a bad storm came one afternoon. Perhaps it was my libido coming to life and girls taking on a different role. Perhaps it was having a few successes in school, especially in geography, or a special teacher who offered to let me take home a set of records to play at home. It was Rossini's *William Tell Overture* on the third record—*The Lone Ranger* theme.

Who knows what it was that replaced the fright with peace and the freedom for me to just be a normal boy?

Beyond the Frightened
Little Boy

AFTER ABOUT FIVE YEARS, THE frightened-little-boy period of my life ended, but over the decades that followed, its aftereffects continued to show up in many ways—one of which was that preachers came to be among my best friends. Let me ruminate about that happenstance, which affected my whole family. The dominant power and peculiarity of preachers in my early life caused me to put them in a category somewhere above the rest of us. They were superhuman. They were unreal. They had the upper hand. I did not like them or the messages they espoused, and they bothered me. I carried a fixation about these characters.

The best way to overcome fear is to face it. We do this as a deliberate endeavor with some of our fears, but we work at others in a subconscious way. With preachers I had to do something so they did not get the upper hand over me. As I matured and became a professional educator, I could stand with them on equal footing. It was a start. I was as good a churchman as I knew how to be, participating vigorously in the programs as a way to compete with the preacher. This unconscious procedure of "humanizing the clergy" has continued throughout my life.

I did not have to seek them out as friends or try to enhance my own life by knowing them—but I did. The list of preachers I befriended is long and notable: Joe Holliday, Julian Cave, and Franklin Ferguson, Episcopal; Bev Jones, Methodist; Charles Hasty, Presbyterian; Kent Anglin, Hugh

Kirby, and Scott Walker, Baptist; Tom Camp, Methodist; Ray Austin, Church of Christ; Buddy Revels and John Claypool, Baptist—and others.

Many people, perhaps an overwhelming majority, go to church and are fine church folks. They do church well and do not sense any need to apply unusual, supportive connection with the preacher or preachers. Why did I? There was a deep need in me to demystify and defrock them in order to take the stinger out of my spirit, which came from my terrifying experiences as a boy. My wife and I began to read their stuff (theology), bought many books on spiritual development, collected sermons, read hundreds of their sermons, visited churches where they preached, and stayed in touch with them. We knew who was saying the things that we needed to hear. We could hold up our part of the conversation with any of them. It did not take us long to find out that there was nothing special or extraordinary about them. They also had feet of clay. They did not really stand above us at all. Their lives were just as scratchy and wobbly as ours. It was simply that they chose to preach as a life profession.

Now, what about the storms that at one time tore me out of my frame and turned me into a zombie? I believe the residual effects of those times later inspired my desire to study space and astronomy. This might be a stretch, but there is a relation between the unpredictability of weather and the Newtonian certainty of the cosmos. However, long before I found the sky, I went through several stages of coming to grips with storms. Becoming a soldier meant living like a man—a soldier just cannot be frightened by storms! When I married, I had to be a strong man and not a wimp about storms. When I became a father, I had to reassure children that storms were part of life and teach them to respect them but not be frightened.

Then, somewhere in midlife, I became curious about the cosmos. I read book after book on the topic, attended conferences, talked to faculty in the field, and served on the program development committee that met with the great Carl Sagan to help him decide to do the fabulous public broadcasting series *Cosmos*. As my knowledge base expanded, I sought new concepts and facts that would help me live comfortably with my fears and anxiety. As I explored cosmology, theology, paleontology, and other scientific disciplines, my sights turned toward what I learned to call "deep time"—that long period in bio-evolution before the rise of civilization and religion. I sought to find antecedents to the development of the myriad stories of creation, which made less and less sense to me as the "new" scientific world came into sharper focus. In combination with this knowledge was my growing awareness of the power of the collective, the amazing, ever-accumulating human imagination and spirit. Questions unwelcomed in the faith communities buzzed in my mind. My goal became to search for answers but also to question the answers I had lived by for too long.

Isn't it a bit odd that I would eventually take the *storms and churchiness* of my youth and wrap them around my great interest today?

The little boy is frightened no longer!

A Hook Shot in the Sanctuary

A FEW YEARS BEFORE ATTILA the Hun became our preacher, we had one who was kind, gentle, dapper, educated—and tall. When the Reverend J. A. Cave walked down the street going to church each day, he had on his flat-topped straw hat and was the picture of gracefulness and delight, but he still represented authority and adherence to strong Christian behavior. He always had a book under his arm. He was very friendly to all. He tipped his hat to the women who were sitting on their front porches in the cool of morning. We held the Cave family in awe. They had four small children. His wife was an extraordinarily pious woman, who always dressed in black as if she were in mourning. Church was serious business to her. "They all get down on their knees after supper every night and have long prayers," someone had told Mama.

The Baptist church and the Methodist church in the village were on the same block, separated only by the community gymnasium. I could see them from our front porch. We could make noise in and around the gymnasium, but the two churches required a certain degree of quiet. They stood there all week, silent as ghostly temples, except on Wednesday nights. That was prayer-meeting time. The churches were not inviting at all—I wouldn't go in there by myself at night for "seventy-eleven dollars."

On the basement floor of the Baptist church there was a water fountain, which had the best, coolest drink of water in the whole village, but it was in the holy fortress. During the hot, dusty days of summertime, once in a while, we would bolster our valor and sneak from the high bushes around the gymnasium over to the high bushes at the back of the Baptist church. We knew there was a window with a broken lock that we could enter through. We all got in without being seen and took turns quenching our great thirst.

Lard, Stein, R. W., Wadd, and I were inseparable; we walked to town on Saturdays to see movies, attended the ball games together, and shared a Pepsi Cola and a bag of salty peanuts. We were good church-going boys, not like some of the other boys in the village, who threw rocks at street lights and broke out windows at the school. We were above such entertainments.

One dusty, hot summer day, after we had pitched horseshoes in the beaming sun at the pit beside the gymnasium and shared a pack of salty peanuts that Stein had bought, our mouths were parched. Nobody had six cents for a Pepsi to share. We went to the unlocked window at the Baptist church so we could cool off our heated systems. After a good watering, we began to walk around in the cool of the church, and we ended up in the sanctuary. The church was silent, ghostly silent. We knew no one was there except the resident ghost who came out and roamed only at night.

All five of us walked up onto the pulpit platform. We were quiet and maybe a little reverent as we looked over the big Bible on the pulpit. It lay open, with a big, bright-red ribbon to mark its place. It was opened to something about, "Let us go into the House of the Lord," I am sure.

Suddenly, as if he had been hit by the Spirit, Stein hit the Bible with his fist and started preaching real loud, mocking some preacher he had heard on the radio. It certainly was not Preacher Cave, because he would never hit the Bible with his fist. We all fell to the carpet in howls of laughter. While Stein continued preaching, R. W. stepped over, removed the velvet piano cover, and started banging loudly on the keys as if he could play it. Wadd rolled up the velvet cover into a ball and took off his belt to tighten it around the cover, making it into a basketball. He ran up toward the pulpit and put a perfect hook shot into the baptistry. Lard and I found the collection plates, and trying to balance them on our heads, pranced down the aisles. There was pandemonium in the sanctuary, mayhem in the Lord's house.

At the height of our "worship service," the double doors flew open, and there stood the end of the world, the end of life as we had known it. Preacher Cave shouted, "Boys! What's going on here? This is God's house! You cannot treat it this way."

We all froze in place. The jig was up. We would be exposed as criminals before the whole congregation, and our parents would know of our escapade within the hour. It would be the talk of the village.

As Preacher Cave stood there glaring at us, Lard and I put the collection plates back on the communion table, R. W. rose up from the piano and moved away, Stein walked down off the platform, and Wadd went down into the baptistry to retrieve the velvet "basketball."

"Don't y'all ever come in here again and treat God's house this way," Preacher Cave said.

We followed him out the doors. No one said a word. He went back into the church and closed the door. We walked slowly back toward the gymnasium, wondering what had happened to Wadd. The back steps of the Methodist church were in the shade. We sat down there, still very subdued and worried. In a few minutes, Wadd came around the gymnasium, putting his belt on, and he smiled when he saw us. He came over, sat down, and said, "I didn't know Preacher Cave could play the piano."

Preacher Cave had gone back into the sanctuary, walked around a bit, and then sat down at the piano and sung a couple of hymns while Wadd was sweating quietly in the bottom of the baptistry. Wadd said, "When he left, I put the velvet cover back on the piano and came out that window. I was scared that he would come and look in the baptistry when he was walking around."

We all went to our homes to wait the next part of our excommunication and hanging.

At home that night I waited for the sky to fall. I waited for the big discussion or the bigger hickory stick, but neither came that night. At church on Sunday, I knew we would be brought to the front of the church and a sentence would be pronounced that we were top-rank sinners who had desecrated the House of God. I felt the preacher was staring directly at me the whole service. *He's just waiting until the end of the service before the purging of five wicked boys will take place,* I thought to myself.

He said *nothing.*

Days passed and time softened into common things again. A few days later, I passed the preacher at the drugstore, and he spoke real friendly to me. We never heard a word about those moments in the sanctuary. From then on we walked around the church with great care. Was he wiser than the greatest philosopher, or was he simply a boy at heart that night? Whichever it was, from that night on I admired him—and that was the end of hook shots in the sanctuary.

"Why Do You Tarry, Dear Brother?"

A. HOWARD WILSON, WHO SUCCEEDED the cool and calm J. A. Cave, always sounded mad when he delivered his standard tirade from the pulpit, enumerating his version of the seven deadly sins. For pride, greed, envy, lust, sloth, anger, and gluttony, he substituted smoking, drinking, gambling, cussing, sassing your parents, running around, and going to picture shows.

I fared pretty well as we all sat there doing our mental checklists, calculating which ones we were guilty of committing. Only one on the list applied to me: going to "them hellhole movies." I had tried rabbit tobacco, that sweet weed that grew in the fields near the woods that could be dried and rolled into a neat cigarette, and I really liked Dot Gilmore, but those did not count for much. Would just one of them send a person down the slide to hell?

We sang hymns with words like, "Why do you wait, dear brother; why do you tarry so long?" It seemed as if every song was a plea to "make it right with the Lord," to "get saved." They were persuasive, unrelenting, emotion-laden songs. Why did I tarry? It was simply that I loved my movies.

Getting saved was a life-changing event, and to prove that you had done it, you had to show that you were doing something or *not* doing something. I knew that for me getting saved meant staying away from "them hellholes." It was the only one of his seven deadly sins I needed to give up.

Going to the movies on Saturdays was vastly more than a diversion or distraction from routine. It was the bright, shining star we anticipated, the highlight of each week. We walked those three miles up the railroad cut, past the old haunted warehouse and the village where the black folks lived. We had a box of popcorn and might watch the newsreel, cartoon, the *Three Stooges* comedy, Buck Jones in *Ride the Wild Wind*, and an episode of the continuing series about Flash Gordon conquering the planet Zotta. Our regular excursions uptown to see the weekly cowboy show were our greatest pleasure. With boyhood abandon we made those days exciting. We were free as a puffy white cloud on a windy day. And that fact seemed to burden some folks, who made direct frontal efforts to get me to respond to the call. *Why me?* There were many other boys who had not given in to the pressure and constant cajoling to get down front, be saved, and officially join the church. Was I some potential menace to the village? Was I a scourge on my family? Hadn't I stood twice on Easter Sunday mornings in the pulpit and played my trumpet, giving a good rendering of "The Holy City" or some other Easter-type song? I guess because I had done that, some got the idea that I was going to be called to preach, and they wanted to speed up the process.

I had heard all the Jesus stuff, about how he had come down to save us from our sins and how he wanted us to come to heaven, so what was I to believe? They said it—why would I not believe it? Still, Saturday morning had more going for it than Sunday morning.

The first preacher I remember was Mr. J. A. Cave, who was friendly to me when I delivered funny papers in the village. He kidded with me when he saw me at the company store. I liked him until one Sunday morning after he had preached; he stepped from the platform to receive those who would come down to be saved during the invitational hymn. No one seemed to be coming. I was sitting on the end of the pew beside Mama. He stopped the hymn-singing to make another plea, staring at me the whole time. Then, as the singing restarted, he walked slowly toward me, stuck out his hand, and took mine, tugging it a bit, and said, "Is this the day, Billy?"

I was embarrassed, and I pulled my hand away and lowered my head. He moved away. About that time I caught the eye of my sister, Louise, who was sitting in the choir. She winked at me. Bless her heart! She knew I needed some relief. I never liked him after that moment.

I felt too many adults with some connection to the church were pursuing me like the "Hound of Heaven" in the works of the English poet Francis Thompson. The next one to bother me was our church choir director and my Sunday-school teacher, who gave us nickels if we could say our memory verses. He was a handsome man who had been crippled by a wreck many years before. He had courted my sister a few times. One Sunday morning, after Sunday school, he asked me to stay with him a few minutes. We sat down at a desk, and he told me how much he liked me and my family, and then he said, "Billy, why don't you go down front this morning and make it right with the Lord?" He went on to say, "Your whole family would be proud if you did."

I was stunned into a deep silence and could not say anything. I sat in the sanctuary that morning feeling as if the entire congregation was looking at me. The invitation hymn started, "Just as I am without one plea, but Thy blood was shed for me." Many verses droned on as I sat in agony. I did not go that morning, because I loved my movies. From that time on, I tried to keep my distance from Mr. Paul Compton, my Sunday-school teacher.

It was one of the Easter mornings when I played the trumpet from the pulpit. I was playing "Sunrise Tomorrow," accompanied by Lucille Thomas, our church pianist and encourager of my musical talent. She was an educated lady, excellent basketball player, Chinese checkers–playing friend of Mama's, the wife of the athletic director for our village, and a very pretty woman. That morning, before we rehearsed, she said, "Billy, after school one day this week, come by my house for some refreshments."

I told her I would, and the next day I went to her house, which was on the avenue where all the mill officials lived. We sat at her dining-room table, where she had her Bible lying open. She said, "I know you believe in Jesus—don't you?"

"Yes, ma'am."

"Do you want to be a Christian?"

"Yes, ma'am."

"Do you accept Jesus as your Savior?"

"Yes, ma'am."

She had the acceptance prayer, holding my hands in hers. Next she asked if I would make it public the following Sunday by going to the front when the invitation hymn was sung. I said I would, and we had some vanilla wafers and a Coke. I left feeling sick inside and wishing I had not gone by to see her. Going to the front meant openly repenting for your sins. Good God, what did I have to repent about? It also meant making changes in your life, and the change I would have to make would be to stop going to movies. I did not go to the front that Sunday, and I tried to keep my eyes off Lucille Thomas. Time passed and "going to the front" lost out to "going to the movies" again.

Another Sunday-school teacher of mine, Mr. Darrell Toby, had a marvelous tenor voice and sang in our choir. You could hear him above all the choir. He was a single man about thirty years old, and at one time he had been called to preach, but that hadn't worked out. There were only about eight of us in his Sunday-school class, including Lard, Stein, and Wayne. Mr. Toby talked to us about what he knew was the main stumbling block to being a Christian—*sex*. He emphasized playing with yourself, which he sometimes called "pocket pool." He even confessed that he had played with himself once in the barber's chair, since he had been covered with the barber's apron. One Sunday after class he tapped me on the shoulder and said he wanted to talk to me about something. "Billy, don't you think today would be a good time for you to go to the front and get saved?" I don't know how I responded or whether I said anything. He was "witnessing" to me, doing what he was supposed to do, but my feeling was, "Like a tree planted by the river of the waters, I shall not be moved." I did not go up front, because movies were too much to give up.

Over a short period of time, the preacher, the pianist, the choir director, and my Sunday-school teacher had all tried to get me to the front, but my movies meant more than all their "witnessing, pushing, and persuasion."

Later, I did go to the front, in the heat and emotional circus of a revival conducted by the super firebrand J. Harold Smith. I guess the unpardonable sin and going to movies and the unrelenting assurance of going to hell got to me. I knew no more what I was doing than I knew the secret formula for Coca-Cola. The next Sunday I was baptized, and from then on they left me alone. I did not stop going to movies, but for a long time I felt I was doing something sneaky and not right.

If the man of today who was once that little boy could whisper into his mind, he would say this: "Listen, little fellow, let me tell you what you will grow up to know about this 'being saved' notion. Some time back in the last glory days of the Roman Empire, there was a man named Augustine, who lived a wicked, debauched, despicable life for thirty years and could not explain to himself why he was such a bad person. He invented the idea of 'original sin.' This means that we inherit sin in our beings from birth, and to justify all this he pointed to the Garden of Eden story in the Hebrew epic. His idea was embraced by the church, made doctrine, and became the cornerstone of the Christian faith. You will come to know that this is malarkey. Although some individuals are aberrant, there is nothing inherently wrong with *Homo sapiens* as a species. There never was anything to get 'saved' about, and I am sorry that we (me in the *now*, and you *then*) had to go through that ridiculous bit of imagination and subterfuge caused by St. Augustine and all his compatriots, who have sustained the deception ever since.

"Hey, fellow, next time we are recycled this way, maybe the human race will have learned that love is our nature, not evil—because that is the way it is, and that is what Jesus said."

"You Are a Heretic"

H E LEFT NO WILL TO be read. He left no bank account. He never owned land. He kept no diary or letters to be read. He never traveled out of South Carolina. He never broke a record nor wrote a book. He never ran for public office. He never saw a major-league baseball game. He did not live fifty years, but Bill Hale had a wife, Mae, and nine children whom he cherished. He is buried in a very nondescript grave in a cemetery where as a young man he courted Mae Howard and where they sealed their lives together with many kisses. I have heard Mama say of him, "Oh, he was a handsome man and loved to frolic."

Over the years, I have heard many people—family, relatives, and friends—say, "Your Papa used to say——" or "I heard him say one time——" and then add some words, most of them not memorable. Oh, yes, I heard many statements like that, but one statement stands out above all the rest.

My brother-in-law Will Vickery was devoted to my Papa. "Billy, your Papa could have been governor if he had had an education," he said. Will and Papa learned much about each other while walking to work and back for nearly two years. Will told me many things about him that nobody else seemed to know or bother to tell me. As they walked along the back side of two mill villages at five thirty in the morning and back home again at five thirty in the evening, through cow pastures—"Watch your step!"—they had more than enough time to chat.

"Billy," Will told me, "your Daddy loved to find a new word in the paper for us to talk about. He said more than once, 'Start every day with a question, and someday you will be smart.' He'd ask me, 'Will, what you think them stars are made of?' or 'Will, how can that old brown cow eat green grass but give white milk and yellow butter?'"

Perhaps this was his gift to me—a legacy of asking questions and learning the fine art of doubting the answers we have lived with every day. *Thanks, Papa!* For years I had silent questions that I did not ask or did not know how to phrase into questions. Some questions led me toward deeper involvement in learning, and some led me toward action to be taken.

We landed on the island of Okinawa in July 1945, after forty-eight days of moving through the Pacific Ocean, zigzagging in order to stay clear of Japanese warships or submarines. My regiment was camped out in tents on a mountain slope overlooking Brown Bay. We were there when two atomic bombs hit Japan and ended the war. A few weeks before that occurred, we had been training to invade Japan in the fall, in what would have been the biggest slaughter of human life in the war. While we were waiting for the next move or perhaps to hear some news about going home, we spent our days and nights just doing army stuff. One morning when we saw the division mail truck coming up the long slope, we sauntered to company headquarters to see whether we were lucky enough to be receiving mail. When the mail-truck driver was getting back into his jeep, I asked him a question: "Is there a band up at division headquarters?"

He replied that there was.

My next question was, "Will you let me ride up there with you?" Without asking anyone in authority for permission, I got into the truck, and in about an hour we arrived at the tent cluster of Seventh Division Headquarters. When I found the band tents, I met a sergeant. "What instrument do you play?" he asked.

"Trumpet and baritone."

"Don't need you!"

I was about to walk off, but then I turned and said, "I was drum major in high school."

He said, "Wait here."

Soon a very nice warrant officer, the band director, came into the tent and asked me how I had gotten up to headquarters and what unit I was from. I told him my story. He said they needed a drum major, he told the sergeant to take care of the details, and the rest is history. Those two questions changed the course of my life forever.

Thanks, Papa!

In the Introduction to World Religions course at Furman University in Greenville, taught by Dr. Haight, I was struggling. The textbook material was beyond my comprehension and totally foreign to any experience I had ever had in school. One day in class I was trying to take notes from his lecture. I was very sleepy, and my head was nodding and bobbing. I had worked until midnight the night before and had not even tried to read the lesson material for the day. Dr. Haight sensed my dilemma and said, "Mr. Hale, you seem to be in deep thought today— what's on your mind?"

From somewhere, out of the grace supplied to the inadequate and ill prepared, came a response—a question. "Sir, I was just wondering—is Christianity going to win?" Little did I know I had set him up for an extemporaneous lecture, in which he waxed with some passion and eloquence for the remainder of the period. As he left the class that day, he nodded his head to me and nearly smiled. From that time on, he seemed to be directing his lectures toward me. When I got my midterm paper back from him, I had not done well. He had this note written on the back page: "Mr. Hale, I am sure Christianity will win, but I have my doubts about you." I think my question had endeared me to him, culminating in one of only two or three Bs I made while in college. Oh, the power of the well-placed question.

Thanks, Papa!

In the spring of 1972, Julian Cave, our well-honed preacher at the First Baptist Church and exquisite thinker, invited one of the near saints of Protestantism to come for a few days of theological reflection and spiritual enhancement. Dr. Elton Trueblood, Quaker, teacher, prolific author, founder of the Yokefellow Ministry, and recognized as one of

America's great theologians, was a warm, soft-spoken human being who was easy to be with.

At the time, I was serving as chairman of the Deacon Board at the church, sometimes referred to pejoratively as the "bored of deacons." I had suggested that Dr. Trueblood be housed at the hotel of the Georgia Center for Continuing Education, on campus, where I was associate director. Over his days there, he spent considerable time in my office, reading or using the telephone and just idling his time away between appointments. We had some good conversations.

After his final presentation at the church, a small group of church folks gathered at the pastor's home for refreshments and as a thank-you to the famed theologian. I was seated next to him on the couch with a couple of others, and a question came bubbling up to the surface of my mind, so I asked it: "Dr. Trueblood, sir, at what point in the life of Jesus do you think he was finally and completely convinced he was the Messiah?"

The question was not new for me. It had been rambling around in my mental space for years, and now I had my chance to ask it of someone whom I respected and admired.

His face took on a frozen stare, his eyes blazed with a how-dare-you! look, and he said, "You are a heretic!"

I was stunned, but the people within earshot at that moment laughed heartily, and I sloughed off the embarrassment and joined in with the hilarity. My question had been sincere, but he had been rather curtly dismissive. Some in the room that night never got over the fun of one of America's theological wizards calling me a heretic. I think my question caught the great man out in the soft sand of theological reality, where he had no traction to ride out an answer. My question still stands unanswered.

Thanks, Papa!

Perhaps there is in each of us a question that we ruminate on all our lives. It is mental entertainment for those in-between-thought times. Wisdom is the ability to process those types of questions, to let them simmer, and occasionally, when they come to a boil, to voice them. Often we dread asking these questions because they might identify us as "dumb" or "not all right."

Recently, in Highlands, North Carolina, while attending a lecture by the innovative, provocative Anglican bishop and author John Shelby Spong, I took the microphone during the question-and-answer session. I posed my question with the full realization that I was taking a stand. I asked a question that had bugged me greatly for many months. "Sir, ever since I landed on this planet, people much like you have told me that I have to get saved—what is it I am supposed to get saved *from*?"

He answered my question with enlightened and refreshing words. "There was nothing ever wrong with the human being, except we have yet to reach our maturity."

I had finally voiced my question. His answer is in the incubator and growing.

When the meeting disbanded, Helen and I found our way to the stage to have the chance to meet in person this man whose books had tantalized us for several years. We waited in line to greet him, and when we got to him, he quickly said, "I did appreciate your question, sir. Thank you."

No one else was in line to shake his hand, so I asked him another question. "Dr. Spong, what do you think God was doing in the affairs of the human being one hundred thousand years ago?"

He looked at me, puzzled, and quickly said, "I don't have a clue."

Again I had been put off by a great thinker. Why did he not give me an answer? Perhaps it was the wrong place to ask such a question. Perhaps he was in "soft sand." Well, just perhaps!

My life with questions has been a marvelous journey.

Thanks, Papa!

Out of the "Holy" Closet

*The recipe for perpetual ignorance is to be satisfied with
your opinion and content with your knowledge.*

YOU CANNOT GO BACK AND do life over again. You just suck
up the past and let it be the way it was. Those things that ring
joyfully and sing their spirit seem to fade in and out of the
memory bank. However, those things that make you cringe when you
recall them stick in the corners of your consciousness like epoxy. There
were several times in my life when the Bill Hale I was then did things that
would be a total embarrassment to me now. If time was not linear and
fixed, and I could jump back and perhaps meet that Bill Hale, I would
find him contemptible and despicable, worthy of scorn.

In the common parlance of current times, those in the "gay" community
speak of coming out of the closet. I think that phrase can be employed in
other facets of life. It took me a long time, much too long, to "come out" of
the rigid, unreasonable, self-righteous morality closet in which the church
had entrapped me. It still continues to trap me, but now it's only with a
faint shadow of its presence. I am "out," and at least I am on my way!

If the current model of Bill Hale could meet, know, and associate
with the Bill Hale of 1948 who was a student at Furman University
and a member of the village Baptist church, he would be chagrined and
mortified at his attitude toward his faith and at his strident morality.

I was sitting one morning in a small, cozy café just off the campus,
having a cup of coffee with a small group of fellow students. We were all

Baptists; Furman was the South Carolina Baptist university. One of the couples had visited an Episcopal church in Spartanburg for a wedding the previous weekend. They talked about the church and said, "They served real wine at the Lord's Supper." I chimed in about the evils of wine and how the Bible did not really mean wine but just grape juice, and said that any church that served real wine was committing a sin in the church. Some of them laughed at me, while others chose not to respond at all. When they laughed, it only bolstered my pomposity in the stern rebuke I had made about this break in morality—in the church, of all places. Today, I would want to simply smack that Bill Hale in the face—my God, how closed-minded, ignorant, ill-mannered, restricted, and self-righteous can you be while believing you are right?

For decades we went to Sunday-night worship services because that is what "real Christians" did. We cut short family recreation, fun, and relaxation to make sure we were there. It was an unwritten ordinance of the family—Sunday-night church! I harbored resentment toward people who did not go to church Sunday nights. I even believed that if a man was elected deacon, he and his family had a Christian obligation to be at church on Sunday night. It was a ritual that pleased God and made Him proud of us. Even when someone in the family was sick and we had to miss Sunday-night worship, deep down I felt we were doing something wrong and God would not bless us. I demanded attendance and I was adamant about it! Sunday-night church was essential to our Christian way of life. If I could, I would now kick the butt of that Bill Hale all the way to the ballpark and back. Oh yes, if I could erase that Bill Hale, I would enjoy it. He was so cocky about church participation; he wanted to be recognized and praised for his loyalty and support of everything churchy. However, sincerity is not a substitute for truth.

One Sunday when our son Billy was about twelve years old, his Sunday-school teacher, a neighbor and friend, asked Billy if he would like to go to see the Atlanta Braves play the Chicago Cubs that afternoon in Atlanta. In the car coming home from church, Billy told us, with delight in his voice, of his invitation "Can I go? We are going to leave about one o'clock."

"Certainly not!"

"But, Dad, he already has the tickets, and I really want to go!"

"We don't go to ball games on Sunday—you call and tell him you cannot go."

Helen gave me a glance, the kind that says, *Are you really saying that?*

I stiffened my resolve, my inviolate moral code, glanced back at her, and said, "He would not get back in time for church."

At home, he made the telephone call. The air at home was testy and void of the normal chitchat. We had dropped by Kentucky Fried Chicken and brought home for lunch a barrel of chicken and all the trimmings. As we were eating, Billy asked in a chiding way, "What you gonna do this afternoon, Dad?"

The silence had been broken, and I answered, "Oh, I will probably watch television—might even watch the Braves."

"What's the difference?" Helen asked.

"All the difference in the world—we will not be there in *that* crowd."

She smiled and laughed. My morality was on the gangplank, about to fall in the sea. Old Dad had been hoist on his own petard, and he knew it. Reason began to rise above the farcical, laughable insanity of the position I had taken, and I said, much to my amusement and later delight, "Billy, someday I might see where I was wrong about this." At least the fool (me!) had not become a total stone pillar of holy stuff! If I could meet that Bill Hale today, I would delight in giving him a series of swift kicks in the pants and a stern lecture on giving up his inane piety.

Of all the Bill Hales I have been, if I had to pick just one to revisit and kick around a bit, it would be the 1960 model. He had finished his graduate work at Florida State University and was on the faculty of the Woman's College of Georgia as an associate professor of secondary education, with a new doctorate, all of which, incorrectly, presumed some enlightenment.

The president of the college was Dr. "Buzz" Lee, a Southern gentleman, a progressive administrator, Presbyterian elder, and good family man who was warm and friendly toward our family. We had played golf together and had dinner in his home—which was the Governor's

Mansion in Georgia, way back in the history when Milledgeville was the capital of the state.

In the late summer of our first year at the Woman's College, on a Sunday afternoon, we were having lunch, probably tuna salad, which was the staple meat in our price range in those early start-up days. The telephone rang. "Bill, this is Buzz. I'm taking the kids out to the country club for a swim and wondered if your gang might want to go with us?"

"Thank you, but we don't swim on Sunday."

There was a long silence. "Okay! Just wanted to include them; see you tomorrow."

Did I really say that? Yes! For hours afterward, I had a private personal seminar on morality and social conduct. I knew I had caused a wrinkle in our relationship. What unmitigated gall! What social stupidity! What religious self-righteousness! I had embarrassed myself protecting my Baptist mentality. Helen asked when I returned to the table, "What was that about?" and I told her about what I had said to my president.

"Why?"

"I don't know why!" I felt the wind was out of my sails and wished I could replay that scene from the time the telephone rang. Today I could take that Bill Hale out to the wood shed and whup him with vigorous delight. I truly despise that model of me. Did I learn from that fracture in my life? Probably, but slowly. It's been a long, long road, and I am still on it. Too soon old, too late smart!

When did freedom come? Perhaps it came when I discovered that the petty "sins" drummed into me over and over—with great warnings of awaiting hellfire—from the pulpits of my youth were not sins at all. The real sins are world hunger, inequality, pollution, oppression, racism, and war. I was dealt a heavy dose of guilt, which I translated into a crazed mental construct. I developed the idea that the less I sinned the more God would bless me and that when I did sin, God would punish me or someone I loved. This insanity of faith burdened me for many decades. Many of my life's actions were bargaining chips with God. The church had made a cripple out of me. I had been dealing with false beliefs—I was a religious basket case. Oh my God! How good it is to walk without that crutch!

Is it a fact that we all have in our personal histories times and circumstances during which, because of our action or words, we were less than we could have been? What better time than now to revisit those moments and learn from them?

Ah, Come On Now!

FOR DECADES I LIVED A "good life." I stayed on the lawful track, in the zone of reasonable and predictive behavior. I grew up, received my basic education, served my country during wartime, went to college, joined my profession, progressed up the leadership ladder, loved one woman, raised a family, made a good living, retired, had an exciting second career, traveled the world, went to church, became a leader there, taught youth and adult Bible classes, donated to charities, participated in the civic, political, and cultural life in the communities where I lived, helped my fellow human beings, and am thriving in my retirement years.

Alongside the *me* of that "good life" there has been another person. He has been a trickster, a questioner, a keenly curious being who from the earliest days would often cause me to put on the brakes in my mind, creating mental skid marks in the gray matter. This activity occurred when someone made a statement that caused my trickster side to say, "Ah, come on now!"

In my youth we had those absurdly long revival meetings every summer for two long weeks, those excruciating "get-saved" church services every night and twice on Sundays with an evangelist from somewhere far off, like Hartwell, Georgia. These revivals were designed to make us uncomfortable, and they always succeeded.

Sometime in my early boyhood, about 1936, the birth of another *me* occurred, and I began to see the world through a duality of personality. I was not schizophrenic. It was not pathological. It was a great discovery.

I had found a place where I could rest in the comfort of questioning the world of answers I had been given without appearing weird or odd. It was a private place, where reason had the upper hand over common, traditional beliefs and practices.

One of the first times I recall making those mental skid marks, I was in a worship service. I was about eleven years old. Our pastor was rendering the morning prayer, which included this phrase: "Now Lord, we know that you know our thoughts before we think them, and you know every hair on our heads."

Stop! Time out! Skid marks in my mind! I dog-eared the moment. *"Every hair?"* I looked up at A. Howard Wilson, who was nearly bald, and thought, *God will not have a lot to remember there. Every hair? Really?* Then my mind went to a scene that occurred every Saturday night at the village barbershop. After a day of haircutting, the floor would be covered with dead hair, cropped from dozens of heads that day. Rob, the shoeshine boy, would sweep it into a pile and dump it. My mind thought, *There's a lot of hair that God can forget about. Every hair? Ah, come on now!*

We never prayed around our house unless it was done in private when we felt the need. Blessings at the table were rendered only when we had company. There were a few notable times when prayers were cast at the ceiling by our preacher, who came calling every once in a while. That man walked the village visiting his flock. When we knew he was "loose" in the village and saw him approaching our street, somebody would shout, "Here he comes." Mama would make all of us gather in the front room. After he had chatted awhile, he would say, "Let us have prayer." He would kneel on one knee and, holding his floppy Bible up in the air, raise his face to the ceiling and say, "Lord, bless this house. Give Widow Hale the strength to raise these children so they will be fine people. Help these boys to walk the narrow path, and keep these girls under your wing. Help us all to gather in Your House every Sunday to worship you. In Jee-us-ses name. Amen!"

He was a good man, and we disliked him immensely and were all glad when he left, because he made us very uncomfortable. Why did he have to remind God that Mama's man had died? "Widow Hale"! What a stupid thing to do. Ah, come on now!

As the years rolled by, I prayed regularly and got pretty good at it, but somewhere along the path, my other *me* began to raise an occasional counterpoint. I know there are some questions that should not be asked. However, I can, from my trickster side, turn them loose. One thought, which had simmered in me for a long time, came to a boiling point: if God hears the prayers of all humans, and there are six plus billion of us, then at any one given moment there could be one hundred million prayers being sent. These prayers range from the pontifical tones of the Archbishop of Canterbury to the quiet meditative words of a Buddhist monk, the blasting verbiage of a street preacher, or the child kneeling at her bedside saying, "Now I lay me down to sleep." This is a great tsunami of words and thoughts being uttered from around the earth. Even if I stop to consider the *omni*s of God—omnipotence, omniscience, and omnipresence—it is a stretch to comprehend that God processes that endless barrage of thoughts. Perhaps I should not go there, should leave that one alone and fall back in the comfort of, "Only God knows!" Well, I want to know! Ah, come on now!

Sprinkled throughout the great Abrahamic Faith Movement's literature are many references to space or cosmic events, which hover between total absurdity and plain ridiculousness. "The day the sun stood still"; "a star perched over the manger"; and "He ascended into heaven." *Skid marks!* These things cannot and did not happen. Then what do they mean? We do not have to apply sophisticated physics to know that these did not occur; it takes only a simple bit of everyday logic to inform the mind. Ah, come on now!

The revivalists of my youth and the regular pulpiteers—most of them having questionable intellectual dexterity—kept before us the threat "unless you repent of your sins you will spend eternity in a hot, burning hell as guest of the devil." Mental skid marks! The marketing concept here is that fire hurts when it burns you. Then they remind us that "to dust you will return." Oh, I get it! I am only a spirit. Would fire hurt a spirit? Ah, come on now!

Visiting the great art galleries of Europe, especially those of Amsterdam and Rome at the Sistine Chapel, we stood before paintings by the incomparable artists of the sixteenth century. Great pieces of art depict the Bible characters and even God Himself! Many people tend to accept these images as the actual reality, as if the artist had been on the scene making sketches. No one has even a vague clue what any of those persons looked like, yet they become fixed in our minds. Ah, come on now—we know better than that!

A young lady stood in our den one afternoon and said, "We decided to sell our house. We prayed about it, and God said we should do it." She continued, "We put it on the market the next day and sold it the following morning—God does wonders." Skid marks! Ah, come on!

This type of thing is prevalent in our country among those who are still in their cocoons and have never taken flight into reality. I can accept religious hucksters like Pat Robertson or the late Jerry Falwell because they are in show business to make their millions and because they use God as their "Buddy" and claim to have a private pipeline into heaven. I can take them because I can laugh at them. But for reasonably intelligent folks to make statements such as, "God will not continue to bless America if we allow gays to roam our streets," or some ill-taught, silly athlete to say, "God was with me all the way in the final seconds of our game—Jesus was at my side and we won." Skid marks! Ah, come on now! That is malarkey, and they know it.

Perhaps I should apologize for letting my trickster side speak, but he has his rights too. He has been the source of distress at times, but he has also been a boon to my spirit. We now live comfortably in the same winds that blow against my nest, where we have learned to ride out and cherish the brisk gust of new information.

To make skid marks, you must put on the brakes!

WORK

The Bulldog

I WAS EXPERIENCING MY SECOND year in the fifth grade—I had failed it the first time, and that was in a school that practiced social promotion—when the announcement was made that there was going to be a school band. I told Mama about it, but knew I did not have a horn to blow, and certainly we could not buy one, and so I forgot about it. The band director was to be a Mr. Gatwood, who was the director of the high-school band. He called a meeting of the parents of interested students. Mama went, and I later heard that Mr. Gatwood told them, "Teach a boy to blow a horn and he will never blow a safe."

One morning when I'd just gotten up and was approaching the kitchen, I overheard Mama and my oldest brother, George, whispering. George said, "Well, let's get him one."

My brother knew I loved the trumpet playing of Clyde McCoy, especially when he played the amazing "Flight of the Bumble Bee." We had both heard him and his orchestra in concert at the Carolina Theater.

Late one Friday afternoon, I was sitting in the front-porch swing and saw George get off the trolley with a black case. As he approached our yard, his smile grew bigger than ever. He came up the steps and said, "Billy, come in here, and let me show you something." He opened the case, and I saw the beautiful gold trumpet. It was mine! The whole family gathered around to look at it. Somebody said, "Blow it." I tried but made a horrible sound. We all laughed. Neither Mama nor George knew at that time how this instrument would set the course of many of my choices throughout my whole life. It would be band, not football or baseball. It would be drum major, not quarterback. It would be music, not sports. The ancient poet Virgil wrote, "As the twig is bent the tree inclines."

Later in life I would become a teacher of world history at Gaffney High School. Gaffney was rabid about its football. It had a coaching staff made up of tobacco-chewing, crude men with little interest in the academic side of school. They were required to teach a couple of courses, which they disliked very much. They never attended faculty meetings. They were "big-time operators" who remained aloof from the rest of the faculty. I disliked them very much!

After three years of teaching, and having earned my master's degree in secondary education from the University of South Carolina, I was asked to be principal of the high school. I was young and inexperienced in managing people, but I was ambitious. I wanted our school to be a better school and to have a more balanced curriculum and offering of student activities. I put some requirements on the coaching staff. They were to attend all faculty meetings and spruce up the field house and dressing rooms, which smelled of dirty socks. I made some suggestions that I thought would improve the essence of athletics, such as placing mirrors in the dressing rooms so the young men could comb their hair after having physical education during the day. I insisted on traveling teams dressing neatly. I asked the coaches to chew their tobacco only on the practice field. The suggestions I made came back to me in cutting, disrespectful remarks that I heard from faculty and students, such as "He wants us to be sissies down here" or, from the head coach, "What's the fat man talking about today?"

For two years I tolerated these disciples of Frank Howard, head coach at Clemson University, who thought they were above the rules and policies of the school. They did little to promote or foster scholarship, gentility, or gentlemanly qualities among our student athletes.

In the spring of the next year, I asked the head coach to drop by and see me one afternoon.

"What you want to see me about?" he asked, with a touch of impatience in his voice.

"Sit down a minute, Coach. Coach, your philosophy and mine just don't match, and I am going to recommend to the board that your contract not be renewed."

The coach was a friend of the school board chairman. He was a former Southern Conference tackle at Clemson University, former professional player with the Philadelphia Eagles, and ten years my senior. He had had a winning record and was a big man in town, but now I was calling him on the carpet.

"Are you trying to fire me?"

"Coach, I think we need to part ways."

"Boy, you can't fire me—you come in here with your fancy ideas thinking you somebody. Does the board know about this?" He was standing there red faced and fuming.

The coach tried to sue me, but it did not get very far. The superintendent and school board supported me, and quietly, so did the faculty. We needed a new coach. Even though I had played the principal role in firing the former coach, I would have very little to do with the hiring of the new coach. Changing coaches was big news in Gaffney, where football was big-time stuff. The process of finding suitable candidates and collecting resumes was the private domain of the school-board chairman and the superintendent, who were former jocks. I would play a very minor role in the selection process.

They narrowed the candidates down to one man. Some weeks later, in the lobby of the Carroll Hotel, the superintendent, the school-board chairman, and I met Mr. Garland Williams for the first time. He was there to be interviewed and hired as our new head football coach. He was known as Bulldog, and he was one of Georgia's great football players of all time.

Williams was a big man, with curly blond hair and eyes a bit close together—he was two hundred and sixty pounds of bulldog. He was dressed in a very smart jacket and trousers. He'd coached at a private school in Atlanta, was a University of Georgia graduate, held a master's degree from Peabody College in physical education, was an all-conference tackle, and had been selected by Wally Butts to his dream team. He had a big booming voice but a gentle countenance. During the interview I asked him, "Why did you choose coaching?"

He sat there a long minute and then, in a priestly voice, said, "I love the game, but I would rather win a boy than win a game any day."

Three Baptist deacons took the bait. We signed him up right there.

A few days before that, the superintendent had asked me to call the prime candidate's main reference, who was the well-known and nationally recognized coach of the University of Georgia's famous Bulldogs, Coach Wally Butts. I got him on the phone, and he told me Bulldog Williams was one of the finest men he'd ever coached. "He's smart, and y'all can't go wrong hiring him as your coach. He will make you proud."

Early one morning, soon after Bulldog arrived in town, Melrose, our head janitor, came to my office to tell me they were taking out the window frames in the field house so they could get Bulldog's desk into his office. It was too big to get through the regular doors. It was a desk that a former coach had given him when he had received a new desk. It was the biggest desk I had ever seen; it was of special value to Bulldog because it had once belonged to the famous Wally Butts.

Anticipation was building in the community and school about the new coach and his two new assistant coaches. It had been customary for the squad and their parents to have a watermelon slicing the day before the first day of practice. I rarely attended these events. On the day of the gala occasion, about four o'clock, I got a call from Bulldog. He was frantic. "Mr. Hale, where are the watermelons?" He'd thought for sure I would take care of that because he was "so busy"! I told him to send a couple of the boys down to Phillips Market and get the melons and charge it to the Athletic Department. Celebrated people sure assume a lot!

Practice started the next day, very early. They had two practices each day. Forty-four boys came out with great enthusiasm. And here is the story I was told later in the day. After a half hour of exercises, Bulldog gathered all of them around him in a circle. The team was in full football gear. Bulldog had on a T-shirt. He asked two of the senior linemen to take a stance in front of him, with these instructions: "I'm going to get down here, and when I say 'hup-hup,' you take me out of this stadium."

He said "hup-hup," but he jumped a bit early and knocked them back on their butts and jumped on top of them, grinding and flailing all over the two boys. One of the boys got up with a smear of blood on his mouth. Bulldog then announced to an astonished group of boys, "Gentlemen, that's called football."

That same afternoon, while I was at my desk working on some final opening materials for school, I heard a loud commotion in the outer office. I looked up to see Bulldog come in panting and sweating, obviously about to lose it. Before I could greet him, he said, "I thought this was a football town."

"What are you talking about, Coach?"

"We had forty-four guys this morning, and now there are only twelve down there for practice—I can't have a team like this."

"Where are the others?" I asked.

"I don't know."

I suggested he go on back to the practice and I would see what I could find out. I called Cecil Drake, who was a student leader and senior on the team, at his home. He answered the phone. "Why aren't you at football practice, Cecil?" I asked.

"Mr. Hale, that man is crazy. I mean *real* crazy!"

"What do you mean?"

"I ain't playing for that fool man!"

"Cecil, what happened?"

After he told me about the scene earlier in the day, I said, "We got to have a team—come on back. The coach probably just got excited. Round up the boys, and come on back."

"If you say so, Mr. Hale."

I had several calls from parents that night at home. About twenty-six boys came back to practice, and we did have a team. They won their first two games playing smaller schools. The third game was against Rock Hill High School, a very fine school and a rival. We lost the game 14 to 0 and were devastated.

It was a long-held tradition that after each home game the team, coaches, and cheerleaders would go to a restaurant for a celebration meal.

This night it was a steak dinner at the Shangri-La Restaurant. When the coaches arrived, a group of boys, among them Dickie James and Robert Delahey, were in the parking lot of the restaurant. Both these boys were troublemakers; one was a student and one was not. They were sitting on the hood of a car, and when the coaches started to enter the restaurant, Dickie made some catty remarks about the coach's lack of ability to win the big game. Bulldog turned to one if his big tackles, "Bull" Bobby Blanton and told him to pull Dickie off the hood and "whip his ass."

Bull said, "Coach, he's my friend."

Then Bulldog said, "You mean you not going to fight for your coach?"

That is when Robert Delahey slid off the hood of the car, walked slowly toward Bulldog, pulled a knife, and said, "Coach, if you want a fight, I will give you this up your ass."

The coach did not come out of the restaurant until the parking lot was empty that night.

I was home in bed, oblivious to the drama taking place at the restaurant. Around midnight we were awakened by loud banging on our front door. When I opened the door, there stood Bulldog, trembling and sweating. He burst out with, "Mister, I am leaving this town; they trying to kill me," before I could even say a word. He was in a fury, beside himself.

I finally said, "What happened, Coach?"

"They pulled a knife on me out at that eating place; are you going to call the police?"

I assured him that the next day I would check it all out with the police. He left, still mumbling, "I'm leaving this town."

It took several telephone calls the next day to find out the story. I did call the police; they already knew all about it and basically dismissed it as teenage stuff.

All the coaches were assigned classes to teach. Coach Williams had two ninth-grade civics classes to teach. Word kept coming to me that in class he always talking about football and his exploits with the Georgia Bulldogs. On a visit to his class one day, I saw a blackboard full of *X*s and *O*s and three boys sitting with him up front while the class read quietly. This was not teaching civics.

All of the teachers were assigned lunch duty, which meant they would roam around and be present where students gathered. One bright, crisp late fall day, the students were outside. There was a big crowd at the horseshoe pit. A game was coming to an end, the score 18 to 19. Bulldog, who was on lunch duty, sauntered up to the horseshoe pit and boldly said, "Let me show you how to really pitch horseshoes."

Whitey Vassey, a sophomore, said, "Aw, Coach, let them finish the game." Bulldog ran like a charging bull, grabbed Whitey by the shirt, and dragged him into the building.

I was sitting in my office talking to the superintendent on the telephone, when I heard loud voices and commotion in the outer office. Quickly I disengaged the telephone call, and then I saw Bulldog. He was shoving Whitey into a chair, and with total disregard for decorum, shouting, "Mr. Hale, either he goes or I go." Whitey started to say something, but Bulldog said, "Shut up, boy."

I asked, "What happened, Coach?"

"He sassed me in front of the whole school! Like I said, Mister Hale, either he goes or I go."

The man had lost it!

At this point, a sane calmness came over me, and I said one of the best lines I had said in my life up to that point: "Coach, I have no reason for him to leave."

Now with rage, he said, "Are you trying to fire me?"

I reiterated calmly, "Coach, I have no reason for Whitey to leave."

Bulldog stormed out of my office and the school, and he never returned, except to get his Wally Butts desk. We later heard that he had been hired as an assistant coach at Stetson University, but they soon afterward disbanded football, and he became an assistant in the admissions office.

I had had it with football coaches. I decided that they should never be allowed to have contact with the high school other than in the field house or practice fields. I learned that they should be kept away from the scholarly and cultural matters in the school because they didn't understand the true nature of secondary education.

Many years later, when I was serving as an associate director of the University of Georgia's Center for Continuing Education, one of my colleagues asked me to meet her in the dining room for a chat because there was someone she wanted me to meet. When I arrived, she was seated with two of her longtime friends, Winnie and Wally Butts, and she introduced me to the famed coach, now retired. He asked, "Where are you from, young man?"

"Mr. Butts, I was principal of Gaffney High School when you sent us Bulldog Williams."

He put his hands on his face and said, "Oh God, I knew I would meet you someday!"

That was all that needed to be said.

I am ever grateful to George and Mama for that trumpet. I would have hated for it to have been a football—I might have gone through life as a coach.

"As the twig is bent the tree inclines."

"No More! No More!"

SERVING AS THE PRINCIPAL OF Gaffney High School from 1953 to 1958 was a high honor and massive learning experience for me. I was young, probably the youngest principal the school had ever had. I became the principal when I was only twenty-six years old. I made many blunders and misjudgments, but I also made some very workable decisions and established some policies and traditions that smoothed the bumpy road. My administrative style was flying by the seat of my pants, trial and error, and work it out as I went. Nothing in my background gave me much guidance for managing a big high school.

Being as young as I was and being younger than the faculty created a situation where advice from the faculty was not withheld. Miss Rose Ballenger was the grand dame of the faculty. I think she came with the building, like the stairs. She had lived most of the American history she taught. "Miss Rose," as she was known, told me within a few weeks of my principal days, "Mr. Hale (she never called me Bill), these young folks will not remember what you say, but they will remember how you treat them—so treat them fairly."

I knew no other way.

My basic approach toward all people was the gift that came with being born into a big family where peacefulness was the standard manner of conduct. I hurt as a boy when there was rancor or discord among my family members. I despised fussing. I did not rest well if there was conflict between any of us. I know there are people who relish a stormy environment, who create a tornado and feel smug and triumphant if someone dislikes them, and I tried to always avoid those people. My educational experience had fostered in me a let's-get-along method of relating. I went the second mile to keep a relationship. I carried the olive branch of peace and went all the way in order to establish and maintain harmony among people.

"Treat them fairly" meant giving the students space to exercise self-discipline and be involved in the management of their own school, and to make no distinction between the haves and the have-nots or the wills and will-nots.

On every faculty there are a special few who develop leading roles in the drama that unfolds in school each day. Evelyn Boozer was a legend in her own time. She was called Miss Boozer even though she was married with a family. She was as good as gold and tougher than gator hide. Each student's grade was calculated to the third decimal. When in class, every student was required to have on his or her person the famed "Boozer Box," which contained one compass, one protractor, and a sharpened pencil. Failure to have it meant five points off the student's grade. Miss Boozer wore two dresses: one was faded red and the other was faded blue; she alternated them each day. Never was there a student referred to the principal's office from her class. No one would have dared to disturb the classes of the no-nonsense, walk-the-straight-line mega-giant mathematician. She came one day to my office for some reason and, while there, took the chance to give me a bit of advice on school management. "Mr. Hale, you are kind and gentle, still young, and some of these boys will get out of line." Then she pointed to a paddle hanging on the wall. "You will have many occasions to use that—don't hesitate."

The paddle was part of my inheritance when I stepped into that office. I had actually hung it on the wall as a relic of days gone by and as a conversation piece. I never expected that one day a boy would step so far out of line that I would actually want to use it—but it did happen.

One morning a teacher attempted to correct a young ninth-grade boy's attitude. He blasted her with a string of sexually loaded, nasty expletives. She escorted him directly to my office.

"Tell Mr. Hale what you said to me in front of the class," the teacher ordered.

He did not utter a word, only stared at me. This infuriated me. He would not speak. After I sent the teacher back to class, I tried to get him to say the same words to me.

"I can't do that, Mr. Hale."

"Yes, you can!"

"Mr. Hale, I can't do it."

I reached for that paddle and told him to bend over the chair, just the way Miss Abrams had to me in the fifth grade for missing eighteen of twenty words on the big Friday spelling test. I whacked him across the butt one time. I felt my entire being recoil. Shame possessed me, and I blushed deep inside.

He looked around at me and said questioningly, "Is that all?"

I laid the paddle on my desk. "Go back to class and act like a gentleman."

When he left, I took that paddle to the outer office, gave it to my secretary, and said, "Get rid of this hideous thing; get Melrose to burn it."

"Are you sure?"

"I never have been more sure of anything in my life!" If I could not maintain discipline without a paddle, I needed to resign. I had better days than that one!

There must be something in the genetic equipment of boys that drives them to write ugly words on toilet walls. The boys of Gaffney High School were not exceptions to this innate habit. They were good at it, and you could not catch them. I had an intense dislike of toilet graffiti. For me it represented a major breakdown in decorum. I patrolled the toilets regularly, and when I saw writing on the walls, I called Melrose, our chief janitor, to remove it quickly, because if you left it there it would spread like some fatal contagious disease.

There came the time, however, when the writing on the toilet walls crept out into other places. I was standing one morning chatting with Miss Kat McSwain. She was another one of the well-seasoned teachers who gave me advice. She would tell me when things were not going well,

"This too shall pass; this too shall pass." That bit of philosophy helped me many times when my spirit lagged. This day we were standing there outside her classroom, and my eyes fell on some writing above one of the lockers. It was an extremely nasty thing about one of the girl students. Before returning to my office, I went by to see Melrose and tell him about what I had seen.

"Mr. Hale," he said, "it's getting bad—that stuff all over the school."

I was suddenly hit with an idea. I told him to leave it there.

The high school's study hall space was overcrowded, and we had to use the auditorium for that purpose. I knew Junie White, who was president of the student body, was in study hall at that moment. Junie was a fine person and excellent football player, who became manager and resident spirit leader for his team when he broke his leg early in the season. Junie's enthusiasm filled the school with spirit, and he was the most popular boy among all students. I went to the study hall and asked him to come with me. We walked to where I had seen the ugly words on the wall, and I showed him.

"Mr. Hale, that's nasty."

"Wouldn't you hate to be standing here with your girlfriend and both of you see that?"

"That's a shame!"

"Junie, what do you think we could do about it?"

He thought a few seconds and then said, "Mr. Hale, leave it to me. I'll take care of it."

That afternoon, I was down at the practice field, watching the last of the workout. Junie came over to where I was sitting and said, "Mr. Hale, can we have a meeting of just the boys during first period in the morning?"

"Sure, I can arrange that."

"Just the boys—no teachers, and I don't want you there, either."

From all over the school the next morning the boys came to the auditorium. My office was just across the hall from the auditorium. In about thirty minutes, I heard chanting, "No more. No more! *No more!*" The boys left the hall and went back to class. I never knew what had happened in their meeting, except from a few reports here and there. Junie never came to give me a report but did ask my secretary to get Melrose to have a lot of rags ready for him after school that day. That afternoon, about seventy-five boys invaded the school with Ajax cleanser and removed all the writing.

Later I got a report of how Junie had conducted the meeting. When they were all seated, he had told them why they were there and then said, "We will have no more of it, and by *we* I mean *us*." He motioned for some boys to stand. He had recruited the biggest boys on the football team for the cause. About a dozen boys stood; they were all big senior boys. "And we are going to be watching, and if we catch you—and we will—you will lick that stuff off the wall with your tongue, if it takes you all day." He then asked how many would stay and get all the writing off the walls that same afternoon. "We will have no more, no more—let me hear you—*no more!*" He had them all shouting to the top of their lungs, *"No more!"*

A young man showed his leadership ability and made a big difference in the school. As a young principal, I grew about a foot taller because I had put into action my belief that students should have a role in school management. For the next year or so there was no writing on the walls on the school. Junie had taught more citizenship in one hour than would be taught in a year in some of the civics classes.

Addendum: Junie White currently serves as the mayor of Spartanburg, South Carolina, and is a very successful business leader there.

Where They Call You "Mister"

A S A YOUNG BOY GROWING up in the village, I was conscious of the differences between the bosses and the other adults. We addressed all adults outside the family as Mister or Mistress (Mr. or Mrs.) but there was a different quality when reference was made to Mr. Turner or Mr. Pruitt. Their *misters* were distinctive and filled with awe.

One block from the mill, up a slight hill, stood the superintendent's house, the biggest, most imposing house in the village. At Christmastime when you walked past that majestic house you could see the huge tree, with more lights on it than you could count, shining brightly through the big, bright windows. It was a source of oblique pride to have such a marvelous mansion in the village where we lived. It was a two-storied white-boarded house with an oversized front porch, nestled among tall trees, well-trimmed shrubs, and a lush, grassy lawn. Compared with the cottages, the word used to describe the houses of the mill hands, the superintendent's home was a castle. The house and grounds were maintained by a black man who was employed by the mill company. He had a push lawnmower to cut the grassy yard. All the yards of those of us who lived in cottages had dirt yards. The house was on what we called "Boss Boulevard," where about ten houses lined Smythe Avenue. It was where educated people lived with their small families. Perhaps a college education was a good way to control birth?

Most folks in the village were basically oblivious to those houses and the people who lived there, but not Mama. She said, "I'd like to live in that house and sleep upstairs so I could look out the windows and see all the houses." Sitting on our front porch you could see the top story of the big house, even though it was on the next street away. She liked to see it, especially in the evenings when their lights were on. How much Mama dreamed of nice things can be measured somewhat by her love of taking a Sunday-afternoon drive with my oldest sister, Emma. Mama would ask her to drive through the parts of town where the most exquisite homes were clustered, McDaniel Heights and a place called Alta Vista. "Go slow, Emmer, so I can see through their windows," Mama would say.

She really wanted a better life and a better place to live. She had dreams beyond her reach. I heard her talk many times about that big house above the mill and how she would like to see inside. She finally got her wish one day, when Mrs. Pruitt, the superintendent's wife, called a meeting of some of the women in the village to plan for civil defense procedures for the village. The fine lady served them refreshments around the big dining-room table. Mama took mental notes of this day and told us about it often, not with envy but admiration.

Papa was a part of the management staff at the mill, serving as paymaster until his death. Whether or not he would have been promoted to a higher level and lived in a house on Boss Boulevard is a bit of wild speculation. He had only a third-grade education. His death at age forty-nine ended that dream. Papa's ability in community affairs and event organization, his bright spirit, and his promotion of goodwill among the people of the village endeared him to the mill officers as well as to the village people. He had been selected by mill officials on one occasion to appear before a legislative committee of South Carolina to plead their case against shorter work hours. He was their spokesman. He and his name left a legacy for the family and especially for me—his namesake.

Going to college or even finishing high school were not in the expectations or language of our family, nor of most of the village families. Only by a timely turn of history was I presented the opportunity for more education. It was my experience of World War II and the monumentally successful GI Bill of Rights, granted by Congress to honor the returning warriors, that made it possible for me to go to college. While I attended Furman University, I continued to work in the mill. After three years I graduated. I had majored in education after a vocational-preference test indicated teaching would be a suitable area to pursue. I was faced with the question, "What shall I do now?"

Deep down in Mama's being she hoped I would stay at the mill and get a chance to become the superintendent someday and live in the big house. Then she would have a chance to live with us in the castle. About a month before I graduated, my boss told me that the superintendent of the mill would like to talk to me. I was mystified by this request. A few days later, I met with Mr. McCall in his office, where he talked about how proud they were of me and how proud Papa would be that I had come back from the war and gone to college. He asked me, "Would you consider going to work for us in Management Training? You could live here. We have a house for you and Helen—he knew her because she had filled in for his secretary once when she was on sick leave—and could start your pay at $4,000 per year." That certainly sounded like a good way to start. It was a compliment to me and my family and a neat opportunity.

I already had made enough contacts with schools in the South to know that getting a teaching job would be easy, and I had a contract waiting for a position at the high school in Gaffney, South Carolina.

In a sociology class at Furman University, I had learned about the Southern textile industry's poor reputation for treatment of employees. It came as surprise to me that I had lived in such an environment and that it was the subject of research studies. Along with this new information, two dramas occurred in our village that affected my attitude toward corporate life in general and the mill in particular. On both occasions, old-time employees were abruptly dismissed without warning, told they were no longer needed, and replaced by young college graduates. One man, feeling distraught, went home and blew his brains out with a shotgun. The other man became depressed and within a few months died of a heart attack. This stunned me and the entire village, but it struck deep inside me and made me think about fairness and kindness.

I was in a position of having to make a huge decision, a career choice between the good pay and opportunities at the mill and the much lesser pay of teaching school. I was weaving in the mill at the time, working on the second shift and finishing my course work at Furman. I had not been a good student in college, because I had no study skills in my background and had poor reading comprehension. The schools I had attended were progressive, meaning they were based on John Dewey's experimental education models, where the emphasis was on building strong relationships with people, not scholarship. I was not expected to go to college nor finish high school, but here I was about to finish college. I was in the awkward position of having to make at least a B in a public health course in order to graduate. I had worked nights, studied very little, and managed to have just below the required C average to get a degree.

Oddly and delightfully, the course was being taught by my former high-school principal, Dr. T. M. Nelson, who had liked me as a student in high school. I made a special report in the class on children's health, which the professor liked. I made an A—my first and only one in college life. I graduated 392 out of a class of 397—which is printed on the back of my degree—but I had a degree!

My loom fixer in the mill was an older man who had known my papa well. The man had served as the scorekeeper at all the baseball and basketball games, which Papa and Mama had never missed. One day we were sitting in the "waterhouse" (that is what all mill folks called the toilet) taking a break. He was smoking a cigarette and letting the smoke come out of his nose very slowly. "Billy, what are you going to do when you finish college?" I told him of my dilemma. It was either remain here at the mill and move into management or go to Gaffney and teach high school. Mr. Ramsey took a long drag on his cigarette, let the smoke come from his nose, and said, "My advice might not be worth much, but you should go someplace where they call you 'Mister.'"

To say that this encounter with my old loom fixer was the deciding factor in making my choice is to overplay the moment, but when I did go to Gaffney and teach, they called me "Mister Hale." Being called "Mister Hale" made all the difference in the world. It caused me to walk taller and with confidence. However, I was still Billy when I went back home for visits.

Mama never got to live in the big house; I had been her last chance. But she was proud of me and said so, obliquely, one day: "Your Papa would be proud of you."

No Longer

All of our todays will become tomorrow's "no longers."

W E HAD BEEN LIVING IN Gaffney several months before I discovered an old, well-worn, rusty sign on the highway leading into town from Union, South Carolina, which read, "Welcome to Gaffney, The Pearl of the Piedmont." I never knew who coined that phrase, but it sounded like something a Chamber of Commerce committee or a zealous, creative newspaper editor would write. Yet Gaffney was truly a jewel of inestimable worth and quality in our family's history.

Leaving the mill villages of Greenville to move to Gaffney, fifty miles and a planet away from the life we had known, was a monumental leap for our young family. Our behavior, attitudes, values, personalities, and character as a relatively new couple were in the formulation stage, and Gaffney would leave an indelible patina on us, which we can readily see when we flip back through the pages of our history and see those eight years with more mature insight. Our lifestyle changed in radical ways. No longer would we gather at our parents' houses on Sunday afternoons with the family, which was a tribal tradition in Southern mill villages. No longer would I pack a lunch and go to work in clothes that would collect mill grease and grime; instead I would dress up like on a Sunday and go to a work where the worst mess would be chalk dust.

"No longers" came at us in waves. No longer would the mill whistle tell us the village time; now it would be the school bell helping us with time. No longer would we pick up the telephone several times a day to chat with family, because living fifty miles away meant long-distance calls, which were costly, especially on a teacher's salary. "No longers" came in major and minor dimensions. One monumental "no longer" for us was the decision to join the First Baptist Church in Gaffney. Baptists in those days, and perhaps even today, transferred their memberships to the new church in the city where they moved to as if they were "passports to heaven." We were Baptists but not First Baptists, which was a different brand of the same product and very different from the brand back in the village. The superintendent of schools, the school-board chairman, and a dozen members of the high-school faculty were members of First Baptist Church, so it made all the sense in the world for us to go there too. The "no longers" we left in the pew at the village church were many. No longer would the fire of hell, wrapped up in an ill-tempered, overly loud, revivalist harangue for an hour before the emotion-filled "invitation" to get somebody saved, be our Sunday-morning worship style. The First Baptist Church was under construction when we arrived in town. Its services were being held at the Cherokee Theater. At our first worship service, we felt as if we were in a concert hall rather than the "rodeo" we had left behind. The opening hymn was "When Morning Gilds the Sky," a grand old tone poem rather than "Nothing but the Blood of Jesus" and other such hymns.

Dr. J. Frank Morris, the pastor at First Baptist Church, was a seminary scholar and a well-read preacher. His sermons were well crafted and designed to challenge us to be better human beings. He emphasized that God loved us and was on our side. The invitation was a quiet, orderly process, void of the antics of threat and rancor that we'd experienced back home. He was also "noon conscious," a most commendable characteristic for any preacher on a Sunday morning. No longer were we emotionally worn to a frazzle and hungry, but we had relaxing time to enjoy fellowship with the people after the worship service before rushing out to satisfy our hunger.

No longer were we identified as attachments to our families: Mae Hale's boy or that Hendrix girl. We were the Hales: Bill and Helen and little Karen. No one knew where we came from nor seemed to care. The freedom to be who we wanted to be, far from the reputations or influence of our families back home, was a crucible, where we ground out how we would approach our newness in the "Pearl of the Piedmont."

No family in this start-up mode sits and discusses "who are we going to be?" They simply, slowly act their way into their new roles on the new stage. A pearl evolves inside an oyster, one precious layer at a time, without much fanfare, and we evolved one day at a time, imperceptibly changing.

No longer would we live in a cash-on-hand financial model; we would have a bank account and write checks, a totally new experience for us. No longer would we have a community bathhouse; instead, our house would have a bathtub. No longer could we talk, as we had back home, with the loose and unpolished language of the mill village. Being a teacher I could not talk like a weaver, because expectations of teachers were high. We did not notice we had changed until we made visits back home, where we found ourselves switching back to the village wordage for comfort. We did not want to appear highfalutin to our families. Our Southern drawl remained intact, but the words and their pronunciation evolved, with emphasis on certain vowels. We no longer lived in "Sou Carliner" but in South Car-o-lina, with a strong, deep-sounding *o*.

We worked with the "no longers." Some of these were easy, but some were tough roads to travel. Switching from the mill to the classroom was easy; moving from a hell-centered faith to a heaven-centered faith was a delightful transition. However, trying to keep in touch with our larger families back home, with too many miles for easy access, was a true test. We were out of the daily information loop with them and silently, unwittingly, lonely. Soon our neighbors became our surrogate family, and we moved on.

The time would come when the "Pearl of the Piedmont" would become a huge "no longer." This was one of those times when we changed from prince to pauper by resigning a very good position and settling for graduate-school funding. Club Eighteen, nine young couples who had much in common, who hung out together for parties, dinners, and special events, would be "no longer." Those fabulous Saturday chicken barbecues for every family in the block, complete with delicious side dishes from the kitchens of some great cooks, would be much-missed "no longers."

No longer would I stand before the student body in assembly as their principal, making comments preceding a pep rally. No longer would I have two secretaries and a private office, a secluded spot to have serious talks with faculty about their concerns and students about their behavior. The biggest "no longer" when we left Gaffney was a place of prominence in the community. In those days, the high-school principal in a small town was a position of significance, right along with the mayor, the president of the bank, the editor of the paper, and the Baptist preacher.

After we had been in Gaffney for eight years, an offer of a fellowship at Florida State University came my way, and a new phase of our lives began. We put five hundred miles between us and our closest friends, the Caldwells, with whom we had vacationed at the coast several times, eaten many meals together, played Careers for many hours, and shared the same church. No longer would we have that closeness.

Many "no longers" leave an emptiness in your life, to be filled with the next array of amusements, routines, places, and people. You have a chance to change some facets of your habits and to consider how you want to think about many things. We experienced this several times, to our advantage. After graduate-school days were over, we left behind in Florida a big bunch of "no longers" that had defined our lives as we had grown, learned, expanded, and solidified. After two years in Milledgeville, at the Women's College of Georgia, we left there, and the "no longers" were extreme and emotional. It was there that we had developed close friends and gotten our first taste of college life, and we relished it. It was a small college, with all the fine traditions and customs, so inviting and enticing.

In 1962, Athens became the final stop on our wanderings. It was a great place to live, reflect, and spend time recalling "no longers" from our treasure chest of "no longers." Often we used them in our chats about the past or to compare with our current state of affairs. The simple words "Do you remember?" can still pull up any number of "no longers" to massage and reconstruct for our delight and entertainment. You do not have to change residences to experience "no longers." They are ever-present, as time and circumstances change.

Every "no longer" serves as a paragraph in your history, and I believe one of the finest attributes in the evolution of the human being is the mental ability to remember and reanimate yesterday's "used to be's" and the "no longers" into the present moments.

If you get to live long enough, the "no longers" become the source of stories, yarns, and legends. I think it was Mark Twain who said, "When a person dies, a great library is closed forever." A story not told equals one less book on the shelf, one less song composed, or one less work of art created.

I once asked Mama to tell me about her wedding.

"Lordy, Lordy, Billy! I can't remember a thing about that."

After I cajoled and prompted her a bit, wonderful stories came cascading from her. One of the most heartrending was how she and my future papa were married and caught the streetcar to go across town for a honeymoon. I was also moved when I heard that they courted in the graveyard on Sundays—the same graveyard where they are now buried. No one in my family had heard these stories before.

If you give people the space and nonhurried time, they will tell you their stories, and they all begin with "Well, in those days," or "Once upon a time," or "No longer did we ..."

Embrace everything you can now because it will, sooner than you know, become a "no longer."

How Wide Is the Present?

ONE OF THE HAPPY PASTIMES of a midstream octogenarian is the wonderful process of taking a walk back through your history and visiting some of the people who decorated your parade. I find myself doing this often, wondering if they are still alive and what they are doing. My pleasure is elevated when I journey there and find a person who was for a brief time a fine source of entertainment or amusement.

While I was in graduate school at Florida State University, I became associated with a cast of characters whose story would have made a great movie. Mr. Tadros, whose first name none of us ever knew, was an Egyptian native and a fine scholar. His field of study was adolescent psychology. He spoke English but not very well. He was tall, with deep-set black eyes and black, wavy hair, and was always dressed in a shirt and tie. One day at lunchtime, he pointed to the white-bread ham sandwich I was eating and said, "Never eat white bread, because they have taken all the nutrients out of it." Another memorable thing about him was that, without a moment of hesitation, he would start interspersing Egyptian words with his broken English. Why I remember Mr. Tadros is not clear, but he hangs prominently in the gallery of my mind.

I recall another graduate student at Florida State University, named Tom Dooley. I kept hearing about him from others but had never met him. They spoke of this neat guy who was a bunch of fun to be around, so I was anxious to meet him. One day I was invited to play a round of golf with three other grad students, and one was to be the elusive Tom

Dooley. I told Helen about the outing; I would finally get to meet Tom Dooley. We both laughed and began to sing, "Hang down your head, Tom Dooley," which was a popular song at the time, and she wished me luck. We played the round of golf and, surprisingly, I did fairly well. I scored better than two of them, but Tom Dooley beat me by six strokes. Tom Dooley was charming and a good golfer—for a man who had only one arm! You can never forget a man like Tom Dooley.

As I peruse the horde of actors on stage with me at one time or another, there are a few who will stop me in my tracks, and I will have to spend time looking at them. One such person still brightens the scenery and takes the spotlight when we are together in my recollections.

As director of the Communications Division at the Georgia Center for Continuing Education at the University of Georgia, one of the first things I did each morning was to walk through the division and say good morning into each office, stopping sometimes to have a chat. One of the divisions was the Art Department, which supplied art slides for television and art pieces for the Film Department. There were usually two artists at their easels because of the great demand for graphics.

One morning in 1966, I stuck my head in the door of the artists' workroom to say a quick howdy but was stopped in my tracks and must have let my mouth drop open. Seated at one of the easels was a real-live hippie. Though campus was filled with hippie types, we had never had one working at the Georgia Center. Each department could hire student workers without the approval of the head of the division; therefore I had never seen this student. Every hippie looked different from every other, yet there was a definite sameness about their clothes, which seemed to be fourth-hand. They looked different by design and deliberate calculation, but they all had excessive hair all over their heads. Sandals were their only footwear, although many wore no shoes.

Our hippie, David Powell, wore a rope as a belt and a short blanket with a hole cut in the middle to put his head through. Many hippies appeared to be dirty. Not David! His hair was long but shiningly clean, and his wardrobe, a bit unusual, was neat and clean. I had seen hippies on the campus and on the streets downtown. The national television news kept us updated on this cultural phenomenon, showing scenes of their activities all across the country. I had never talked to one, never met one, and never been close to one. Now I had one working just down the hall from me. I was acquainted with some of their phrases—which included "the 'now' generation" and "turned on"—from some books I had been reading. The "now generation" and the "turned-on" folks had penetrated our workforce.

One of my first encounters with him, when I walked into the art room one afternoon, was truly memorable. As I approached his work area, I asked him, "Now, who are you?"

"Hey, man! I'm David—you must be the big cheese."

"Well, yes! I am Bill Hale, Associate Director of the Center. Welcome."

"How nice—do you like your job?"

Nobody on the staff had ever asked me that before. I was immediately intrigued by this anomaly, this abject rarity, this different brand of human being.

Over the next few weeks I dropped by occasionally to chat with David. On one of my visits we drifted into the topic of religion. He had seen in the local newspaper that I was teaching the youth of First Baptist Church a course in sex education, and he commented, "Man, that's real hip!" In that conversation he volunteered, "I'm a Jesus man, and you are a church man."

I felt as if I had been "put down" but didn't know why. "What do you mean, a 'Jesus man'?"

"You know, all the red letters—that's all I need—just the red letters."

He was referring to the red-letter edition of the New Testament, in which all the words of Jesus are printed in red ink. I let his comment about me being a churchman slide by without comment because I had a pretty good idea of what he meant. David was "turned on"!

On another visit, I pursued our chat further. "David, when y'all talk about the 'now people,' what do *you* mean?"

He pointed to a stool and said, "Sit down a minute, sir." Without hesitation, he said, "Let me show you." On a clean sheet of art paper he drew a big square, about a foot in size, wrote a *P* inside, and said, "That is the past." Then he drew another square of the same size, joining the first one, wrote an *F* inside it, and said, "That is the future." He turned toward me and intoned, "You tied-up folks (pointing to my tie, which was standard dress for me at work) have one foot so firmly planted in the certitude of the past and the other one so delicately planted in the ambiguities of the future that you become nonoperational—not me!" Then he drew another *P* square and another *F* square but left about a foot between the two. In that space he drew another *P*. "You see, man! I'm pushing the past back and holding the future off, so I can have some running room to be *right now*—the *present* is where I hang out!"

I felt as if he had preached me a sermon. Then, as a crowning touch to his "sermonette," he looked directly into my eyes and asked, "How wide is the present?"

I had never heard that question before. It was provocative and it prickled.

I understood what David was saying, and it gave me a better grasp of the themes in several books I had read on existential psychology. My speaking career was blossoming at the time, and a common topic was human awareness. My session with David gave me a great story with which to illustrate one of the major points in my presentations. His challenge to me became a standard element in and also the title of one of my speeches: "How Wide Is the Present?" David graduated and left the university, and I never heard from him again. He had faded into that misty world where all graduates go.

My public-speaking engagements took me into many of Georgia's school systems for in-service training days. Once I was in Douglas, Georgia, speaking to the teachers of Coffee County, and I included the story of me and David in the art room in my presentation. Afterward, several teachers came up to chat with me. One young man stood some distance away until all had spoken to me. He was tall and well groomed, with his hair pulled to the back of his head in a ponytail. *Where have I seen him before?* I pondered as he walked closer, and then I knew. "Dr. Hale, sir, I am your David!" We embraced.

"David, I've never forgotten that day in the art room and have told our story all over the country—I hope you don't mind."

He smiled and quipped, "It is a good story. Have we made a lot of money?"

I drove away that day knowing that in at least one high school in Georgia some students are being "turned on to life" because they have a "turned-on" teacher. Thanks, David, for one brief, powerful, shining moment when *you* were *my* teacher!

Ted and Me

OUR INTRODUCTION TO TELEVISION STARTED when we lived in Gaffney, South Carolina. We had an aluminum television antenna on top of our house, strapped with metal bands around the chimney. It was oriented in the general direction of Charlotte, North Carolina, where there was only the one station, WBT-TV. It was 1950. Much later, when we lived in Athens, the antenna was oriented toward stations ABC, NBC, and CBS in Atlanta, and there was also the University of Georgia's Public Broadcasting Channel, WGTV. These were the VHF channels, meaning very-high frequency, and they were assigned channels 2 to 13. There were also, in Atlanta, two UHF channels, which meant ultra-high frequency. In order to receive these signals, you had to have a special attachment to your antenna. One of these stations was owned and operated by the Atlanta School Board and the other, Channel 17, was owned by Turner Broadcasting Systems. These UHF stations were powerful, but their signals were limited to a very small area; they barely reached beyond the city limits of Atlanta.

In 1965 I was promoted to the position of associate director of the University of Georgia's Center for Continuing Education. One of my assignments was serving as the station manager of the public television station, WGTV. This station was a VHF station, and we broadcast a very strong signal all over north Georgia, including the city of Atlanta. We broadcast at every institution of higher learning in the nation with a VHF signal, and the university was proud to be one of them.

Ted Turner and his company owned and operated Channel 17, one of the two UHF stations in Atlanta. He was a multimillionaire, having inherited a media company from his father when he was twenty-four years old. He bought many radio stations in the South and was a media mogul by the time he was thirty. Ted Turner was a world-class yachtsman and a contender several times for the coveted America's Cup. He was known as an inventive, progressive businessman. He was on many lists of the young men to watch in the United States.

One September morning in 1974, when I arrived at my office, I asked my secretary, Nancy Flanagan, as I always did, "What's on my appointment book for today?"

She told me, "You have an associate directors' meeting at ten o'clock this morning, and the only other thing is a meeting with a Mr. Turner at two o'clock." Mr. Turner's office had called the week before and made the appointment.

I knew a Robert Turner in Atlanta, a man I had met at the Center for Disease Control while making a speech there some time ago. He had mentioned the possibility of inviting me to make a speech for him someday. I had this man in mind as my two-o'clock appointment.

I left my office to make my morning round through the division, and as I was walking down the hallway to get a cup of coffee, I passed our station's program director. He reminded me that he wanted me to tape an announcement concerning our FCC license in the afternoon. "It will need to be after about three o'clock because I have an appointment at two with a Mr. Turner."

"What Mr. Turner are you meeting?"

We were passing my office, so I quickly asked my secretary, "What is Mr. Turner's name I am meeting this afternoon?"

She looked down at her appointment book and said, "Ted."

With disbelief in his voice, Hill Bermont said, "What does Ted Turner want to meet you to talk about? Most people I know go to see him."

"I don't have a clue."

He then proceeded to give me a quick tutorial on Ted Turner. This was helpful because Ted Turner had not been on my radar screen except for an occasional mention I'd seen in the papers. My interest was spiked concerning my appointment with such an illustrious man.

At two o'clock I was talking on the telephone. Nancy came in to say, "Mr. Turner is here—do you want me to bring coffee?"

"Let me ask him." I went outside to greet him. There were two other men with him, all dressed in very sharp business suits. I recognized one of the men; the other I had never seen before. "Can we bring you coffee?"

"We just had lunch, thank you. You must be Dr. Hale," he said before I could introduce myself.

"Yes, sir."

Then he introduced Norman Underwood, his lawyer, whom I had met before in another venue, and a Mr. Johnson, whose first name I did not catch. I motioned for them to come to my office, and I took my seat at my desk. The others sat down; however, Ted never sat down. He got right to the point.

"Aha. Mr. Hale, I own channel 17 in Atlanta, and I came over to see if you would be interested in exchanging channels with me."

That caught me by surprise. He smiled as he paced the floor. He paced like an animal in a cage. He smiled like a man who had a great idea and knew I would like it also. Ted Turner was ambitious to reach a wider audience, to make a larger impact on Atlanta, but he was limited by his UHF station. He wanted to be able to compete with the big national stations in Atlanta. Again before I could respond, he said, "I will construct the highest tower in Atlanta that the FCC will allow and put both of us on it." He paused. "And I will give you enough money to completely colorize your station, plus fifty thousand dollars." He was on a run, still pacing and talking and then, under his breath, with a wry smile, he flippantly said, "And we can leave you some down at the park"—meaning that I could benefit personally from the exchange. I am sure this was a tongue-in-cheek comment; nonetheless, his lawyer, Norman Underwood, whose wife had worked in my division as a student, blushed and closed his notebook.

Ted Turner continued, "Do you like the idea?"

I told him I did not like the idea because I believed the university had a chance to make a major impact in our area and that our freedom from commercials would bring us a growing audience. "But, Mr. Turner, I am only the station manager," I said. "There are many others you can talk to about this."

"But *you* don't want to do this?"

"That's right, sir!"

Immediately he changed the subject. "Is there any way I can get *Sesame Street* for Channel 17?" He went on to tell me that it was his kids' favorite show. "I program an hour of cartoons each morning just for my kids, and it would be nice if we could replace them with *Sesame Street*."

I said, "There might be a way, and if you would like for me to pursue the idea, I will."

The meeting was over abruptly. "Thank you for your time—and you are sure you don't want to consider exchanging stations?"

We all shook hands, and as they left I reminded him, "Mr. Turner, there are several administrators here at the university with whom you could talk about this."

He smiled and said, "You've been good to see us—thanks." Ted Turner left and never mentioned it to anyone. My admiration for him soared. He had respected my opinion and my position.

Two years later, he announced his astounding plans for Channel 17 to become the second "superstation" in the United States, following the lead by WGN in Chicago. This would put him in position to create the amazing Turner Cable Network and eventually CNN, the world's first all-news network. He would also be named Man of the Year by *Time Magazine*.

I know it is but silly conjecture or mental wandering, and probably foolish, but I do wonder if turning down his request to exchange his UHF station for our VHF station could have been the catalyst to move him in a different direction. If the exchange had occurred, would the university station have become the first educational television station to take a ride along with his superstation? Is it possible he wouldn't have developed the great idea of CNN?

Never underestimate the action in any one moment of time, because it could lead to an idea that changes the course of history. Ted Turner has no reason to remember his visit with me that afternoon, but I will never forget that moment. It could be that I had done him one of the best favors he had had in years by resisting the idea of exchanging stations and causing him to then look to other ideas for expansion. However, it did give me a good story to tell—about having met in my office one day one of the leading philanthropists of modern times.

Better Than the Next One

AFTER THE FINAL SESSION OF my Advanced Multimedia Methods class in summer school of 1960 at Georgia State College for Women, a student stepped up to me and asked whether I would consider making the opening address to the faculty of Jefferson County Schools in September. Thus began several decades of public-speaking activity. A new thing had come into my life, a thrilling, fulfilling thing that added dimension and definition to my already good journey. As an avocation, along with my regular assignments, public speaking significantly changed the rhythm and economy of our family. I made hundreds of speeches throughout the country and had a wonderful time. However, as someone once said, "If things can go wrong, they will," and they did several times in my speaking days. Bizarre, stupid, and laughable happenings decorate my memory and cause me frequently to go there and relive a moment.

Early in my Georgia days, before I'd learned the map very well, I was invited to speak at a county-wide parent-teacher association meeting in Thomaston, Georgia. On the day of the engagement, I drove to Thomaston, arriving about forty-five minutes early. I stopped to get a Coke, sat for a few minutes, and checked over my speech outline. I went to the high school where the meeting was scheduled to be held. To my dismay, there was not a car in the parking lot! I saw the janitor about to leave. I hailed him down, "Is there a meeting to be held here tonight?"

"Mister, if they is, nobody told me about it."

I went back to my car because I had decided to call the lady who had invited me, to make sure I was at the right high school Before I went to find a telephone booth, I looked in my notebook to make sure the meeting was at the high school and saw—*holy crap!*—I was supposed to be in Thomson, Georgia, not Thomaston! There is no adequate word in the English language to describe my disgust. I found a telephone booth to call the lady and tell her, "I am in Thomson. I have made a great mistake—I am three hours from Thomaston, and I am very sorry and embarrassed." I felt her disappointment, but she tried to make me feel okay about the utterly stupid mistake.

The second-most embarrassing call that night was to my wife, Helen, back at home, to tell her the stupid thing I had done. In her delightful, witty way, she said, "Well, come on home and I will listen to your speech here."

Some very strange things happened when I was on the platform circuit! Bomb scares have interrupted my speeches, and we have had to evacuate the hotels. At an annual conference of the Florida School Food Service in Orlando, a ten-foot-tall block of ice that had been carved into a huge 25, fell as I was giving my keynote speech, ripping down the curtain behind the head table and scattering ice all over the arena. We were all stunned, but I said, "I rigged that up to happen so all of you could have a souvenir chunk of ice." That brought laughter and relief, and I continued with the remainder of my speech.

On the circuit I have been introduced to audiences in many different ways, by many different people, in creative ways. Some were overdone beyond reason and some not at all appropriate. However, the one that often puts my mind in gear is the introduction I received at the American Nurses Association in Denver, Colorado. A fine lady stood to introduce me and read a very long biographical sketch of a speaker who was to address them the following day. When I got to the podium, I made this comment, "I don't know who you were talking about, but I sure would like to hear a speech by someone so qualified." I proceeded to make my speech without an introduction. Strange as it may seem, most people there never knew of the mix-up. Go figure!

There were times when the administrative team at the Georgia Center for Continuing Education worked until noon every Saturday, primarily because if the director, Dr. Hugh Masters, wanted to call a meeting, we had to be there. We usually wore business attire, as we did each day, but occasionally we would dress casually on a Saturday. One Saturday morning when I was wearing casual dress, I was seated at my desk. Suddenly, one of the conference coordinators, Spurgeon Richardson, ran into my office with panic on his face. "Hey, man! You have got to help me. I have three hundred members of the Georgia Federation of Women in the auditorium, and their speaker just called. He's had a wreck in Winder and cannot get here. You gotta come and help me!"

In the years since coming to the university I had developed a couple of speeches, which had been well received, and I'd had many opportunities to present them around the state and also to several conference groups at the Center. In all honesty, in those days I had one theme, one speech, but I varied it a bit for different audiences. I had become a default option when speakers did not show up or could not get there in time because of flight delays. The conference coordinators knew I was willing and available and free.

"But I don't even have a tie!" I said.

He gave his tie and borrowed a jacket from Dr. Bill Brown in the office next door. I walked out onto that stage as if I were supposed to be there in the first place. In the auditorium that morning was a lady from Homerville, Georgia, named Edith Adams. Let me tell you about Edith! She was a member in good standing in several organizations who held their annual meetings at the Georgia Center, and she had attended several conferences at the Center in recent months.

When I went to the podium to speak, I noticed Edith Adams sitting in the front row, grinning like a Cheshire cat. As I spoke, she was mouthing every word I said—she had memorized it. I decided not to look in her direction and deliberately spoke to other faces.

I finished my presentation, and it went well. The applause was generous, and many of the ladies came up to speak and thank me for filling in for the delayed speaker. I noticed Edith standing to the side, waiting for the others to finish. Soon she walked to where I was, smilingly thrust out her hands to clasp both of mine, and said warmly, "Young man, I've heard you speak before."

"Yes, ma'am, I sensed you had heard me speak before."

"But I want to tell you something—each one of your speeches is better than the next one."

"Well, thank you, ma'am. I appreciate that very much."

I left the auditorium feeling pretty good about my opportunity to speak to such a significant Georgian group. It did not register in my mind exactly what Edith Adams had said to me until I was driving home—"*better than the* next *one*"? I nearly ran off the road. Had I heard her incorrectly? Did she really mean to put me down? Was I getting worse all along? I had become so accustomed to hearing what I wanted to hear that I might have missed her message. Thanks, Edith—I think!

MISCELLANY

Colossus

L ONG BEFORE OUR HOUSE WAS built, before a real-estate
salesman sold the land for a home site, the great oak tree owned
this place. When the landscapers came in with their bulldozer
to clear the square acre of land for the house to be built, they'd surely
said, "We better leave this one." *This* was the oak tree, which dominated
the front yard of our home. There might be a tree with more majesty in
this county, but I have not seen it. "Colossus" stands alone as the tree of
significance in our corner of the world.

I named him (I wanted it to be male) Colossus after that word caught
my attention as part of the title of a poem. It was one that Emma Lazarus
wrote, which won a competition as the best poem to describe this nation's
appreciation to France for that magnificent gift, the Statue of Liberty. This
was for the centennial celebration of American Independence in 1876. Part
of the poem is inscribed on the base of the statue. It says, "Give me your
tired, your poor, etc." Colossus graces our yard just as the Statue of Liberty
does the New York Harbor. Colossus is the finest, grandest display of
nature on our side of town, except for the Oconee River. He has observed
the antics and movements of our family for more than a half century. He
is old enough to be my grandfather, who was also a force to be considered!

My relationship with Colossus took a quantum jump when I spent
months planting monkey grass, one plant at a time, under his skirt. It
looked like a bright-green carpet, and I could tell Colossus was pleased
to have such a neat, cool place to cast his shadow. I love carpet in my
house—why not let him enjoy the same delight?

Colossus stands eighty-five feet tall. His family of limbs spreads out into a circled home as big as one of the rings at a Barnum & Bailey Circus. Each year those limbs birth hundreds of thousands of "grand-leaves," and they put on a green dance fit for the opening of the Olympic Games. A horticulturist who visited us said the root system under Colossus reached deep into the earth and probably a half million tiny roots sucked up moisture and nutrients. That would probably amount to one ton of water a day, and a large percentage of that water would be released each day back into the air. That is an amazing gift from him to us every day— fresh, clean, odorless air.

Our huge monument to nature has more character than most human beings. He is proud but never boastful, strong but not vicious, powerful but not pushy, and he never complains but endures in silence the vagaries of life. Colossus stands solid in the fiercest storm, pushed about by wild winds, plummeted by hail, rain, sleet, and snow. He agonizes over the heavy ice that tears away parts of his family, and he hates the summer droughts.

Squirrels build their nests high in his crown and play their comical games endlessly throughout his house, but he delights at their antics: "Hey, guys—it's getting dark! Let's settle down, go onto our nests, and we will all take some rest." Great families of mistletoe attach themselves to his arms and get a free taste of the nutrients pulled laboriously from the deep, hard-packed red clay a hundred feet below. But they are welcomed because they add a nice bit of ornamental detail and intrigue for us.

I habitually speak to Colossus early in the morning as I saunter out to get the mail and newspaper. I hear a breezy *howdy* coming from beneath his arms, still drooped down in a sleepy mood. There are times when I step over and lean my back against his huge trunk, which is bigger than a circle of arms of three adults, and I feel the surge of nature's spirit coarse through my being. His great strength is transferred to me! This is not a one-way process, however. I instill in him the power I have of self-awareness and my ability to know the amazing connection we have. Since we are both made of atoms that are identical in basic construction, Colossus and I really are "atomic cousins" and "genetic copartners" in life's evolution.

Every year in our front yard a mighty, incredible drama takes place in super-slow motion. It is a natural ballet, as thousands upon thousands of leaves twirl and pirouette in an epic production. This "tree-act drama" lasts for a year; it begins in the dead of winter, when the stage is set. Colossus simply waits for the action to start. He is stark naked, cold, and skeleton-like. The first act begins with the birth of the actors by the thousands, who go through their metamorphosis from tiny reddish buds to bright green "flag-ettes," and they dance. Oh, how they dance! Colossus directs the whole show with unwavering skill. Then the second act starts, when each cluster of actors produces tiny round balls to make the dance more interesting. Each of these tiny balls mysteriously contains the code and script for reproducing another Colossus.

The final act is the major production piece. When the food source dwindles, the actors put on dazzling costumes, including most colors in the light spectrum; they catch the autumn sun and sing, "Look at us—aren't we grand?" As the act reaches its apex, the colorful flag-ettes pull loose of their mooring and dive into the air—"whee!"—and settle on the green carpet, shouting back to those reluctant to dive, "Y'all come on—you will not believe what fun it is to turn loose!" At the end of this act there is the amazing and profound climax. The acorns finally fall by the thousands. They fall straight down and take their places, waiting on squirrels, chipmunks, and large birds to feast on them or bury them. The curtain usually falls with the first frost, and Colossus awaits his next "tour."

Every year, dozens of infant oak trees sprout up in the monkey grass, seeking their place in the great oak tradition. Sadly, they are all executed by the weed eater before they can learn to defend themselves.

We, Colossus and I, are taking on the signs of being in our last trimester of life. In this phase one tends to become more philosophical about existence. We have been friends for a long time. Several years ago, I tacked onto his trunk a set of ceramic face features: a nose, two eyes, and a mouth, and it gave the old guy a bit of cartoon-like personality. It was a bit of humanness, but it dawned on me later: *What an insult to the "treeness" of Colossus.* Let me paraphrase the poem of Joyce Kilmer: "I think that I shall never see a poem as lovely as a tree"—nor I a tree with more majesty than Colossus!

Colossus will probably go on living for a long time—hopefully, I will also—but when I'm gone I hope he will think: *I don't know what we are supposed to call them, but he was a real good one.*

Come by and visit him. Colossus would like that!

Old Ben

IN MY EDUCATION, I HAD missed many of the great classics of literature, among them Herman Melville's *Moby Dick*. In 1948, while a student at Furman University, at the insistence of my English professor I attended a special event. The fine British actor Charles Laughton was performing. His readings were electrifying, but the most memorable for me was an excerpt from *Moby Dick*. He made that great white whale come alive, real and alive. Earlier in my own life, another grand fish had created a stir on our village. It was not as big as the great white whale, but the story was a whopper!

"Just stay away from that dirty old mill pond and that junk pile." This was an often-repeated caution rendered by village parents to their children. The junk pile was at the rear of the mill. It was where the mill crew tossed all the used metal after it was worn out. We would sneak down to the pond only when we needed a "steelie," which was a big roller bearing we used as a shooter when playing marbles. Some of the "mean boys" in the village went there at night to toss metal in the mill pond, which was next to the junk pile. The mill pond was a fenced-in square pond, with a flat fountain in the middle that hardly ever bubbled. The water was a deep blue most of the time, until a new batch of waste dye was released into it from the mill, and then it might be red or green.

"Don't ever go inside that fence—never ever!"

Living in the pond was a fish as ominous and elusive as the Loch Ness monster. It was Old Ben. Folks who lived near the mill pond said they heard Old Ben yelling at night sometimes. Often to get youngsters to behave they threatened them, "Old Ben is calling your name." The sound they heard could have been a rusty weathervane on top of the mill, but no one knew. Old Ben was two feet long and had only one eye, and he was mean. Most people believed it was a catfish. I never knew anyone who had actually seen Old Ben, but some had seen the water move and splash, swearing that it was Old Ben. We all knew Old Ben was there. One summer weekend the "Old Ben" story became less a story and more a village-wide event.

One of my best pals was Lard Mason, a kind and gentle daredevil. Over the years he led me into a lot of trouble, not real bad things but things Mama did not like—things like sneaking out of the village to swim in the wash hole we had made by damming up a creek at Chapman's dairy, or finding Indian cigars along the railroad cut and smoking them.

The sun rose on the back side of our house, making the front porch a cool place to be in the mornings. It was a Saturday morning, and Mama and I were stringing green beans for lunch, when I saw him coming down the street, sauntering as only Lard could move, not in a hurry but going someplace. Mama observed, "Here comes Lard."

He and I spent our summer days together like the trees in a forest. We invented having a good time. He walked up the steps and said, "What you doing?" He pulled up a rocking chair and helped us finish the beans.

"What y'all going to do today?" Mama said.

"We going to go fishing," Lard said.

Mama laughingly and dismissively said, "Catch a big one." She knew we were not going fishing; we did not even have a pole.

Walking down the steps, he whispered, "I got an idea."

I told him not to talk until we were in the yard, because Mama might hear him and put brakes on his idea.

"Let's go catch Old Ben," he said.

It was a July day, bright and warm, and now it had turned exciting. In the next few minutes we had sneaked some bread from his kitchen and gotten his sister's big butterfly net. We walked the back alleys toward the mill. Nobody saw us as we cut through the wooded area behind the mill. The closer I got to the mill, the more I heard voices saying, "Stay away from that old mill pond; it's dangerous down there."

There was a huge maple tree next to the fence that surrounded the mill pond, and one big limb extended out over the fence and hung slightly over the pond. That day the water in the pond was bright blue, bluer than the sky. Lard quickly climbed the tree and dropped down inside the fence. "Hand me the bread and that net, and come on over," he said.

I knew we were going to end up in the penitentiary.

With increasing reticence, I climbed out on the sturdy limb and dropped down onto the small patch of grass at the pond's edge. We heard a car coming up to the back of the mill and promptly fell flat on the grass; we knew that if were seen we would be hung on the lawn of the mill for everybody to see. "Let's get out of here," I said, but Lard sat down and started making little round balls of bread.

We had never seen Old Ben, and secretly I hoped we would not see him that day. Lard tossed a bread ball out to the middle of the pond, where it floated a minute, and then suddenly there was a swirl of water about that ball of bread, and it was gone. Lard whispered, "It's Old Ben!"

Fright ran up and down my legs and I repeated, "Let's get out of here."

For an hour we sat there tossing bread balls closer and closer to where we sat. Each time the bread ball would float a moment and then there would be a movement of water, maybe a small splash, and it would be gone. Closer, then gone. Closer, then gone. Next, we saw what looked like a fish tail come out of the water. Then came a splash I will remember all my life. Old Ben jumped high and took a bread ball, and sure enough, I saw that he had only one good eye, and it was red. We stood up, and Lard tossed a bread ball very close to the pond's edge. Old Ben rose slowly to the surface. He hesitated and stared at us.

Don't go near that old millpond!

Lard said, "Hand me that net." Quick as a flash, he dropped the butterfly net over Old Ben's head and jerked. The fish was at least two feet long, with gray and white scales shining bright. Old Ben jerked back, and the net was pulled out of Lard's hand. The fish swam away with the handle sticking up like a submarine's periscope.

Old Ben was gone.

We jumped back up on the limb and down the tree. We did not catch Old Ben, but we had seen him—what scared me was that Old Ben had seen me!

The next day after church, people were gathered outside under the trees talking about something strange happening down at the mill pond. Lard and I had told Stein the night before what we had done, and the three of us listened and joined in the speculation about what was going on down there. That afternoon, dozens of folks were crowded around the fence at the mill pond.

"There it is!"

"What is it?"

"It's a monster."

"Where did it come from?"

"You can count on it—it's that Old Ben."

I was standing beside my mama and two of my little sisters. They had come down to see what was happening. Suddenly, right in front of us, we saw a stick slowly moving across the water. My sisters hugged Mama's legs in fright. The stick would come up and then disappear. I knew, but I would never tell them that it was Old Ben with a butterfly net hung on his head. Even a few of the big bosses at the mill were there at the fence, mystified along with everybody else.

For weeks people came, hoping to see the strange happening at our village mill pond. The local paper ran an article about it. Some days that strange stick would be seen but not all days. As the weeks passed on, it ceased to appear; however, the cautioning of all the boys and girls never ceased: "Don't go near that old mill pond."

We didn't catch Old Ben that summer Saturday morning, but we had seen what he looked like. The story of the moving stick is still told all over the area, mainly among the older folks, but nobody believes them. "Aw, they just made up that story to frighten kids."

The mill pond is now gone. It is filled with sand and dirt, and grass grows there. The fence is gone. Somewhere under all that is a skeleton of Old Ben along with the remains of a butterfly net.

For one bright summer day in my boyhood Old Ben and I were center stage, and along with Lard, we generated millions of moments of human wondering.

The truth can make you free, even with a wink!

Melville told one enormous tale in his book about a huge fish, but for the village folks back in the imaginative days of my boyhood, it was no bigger than Old Ben!

"I'll Be Back": A Healing Fantasy of Imagination

THE WIND WAS BLOWING FAIRLY briskly that cold Friday afternoon in January 1934. There was great commotion in the hallway and outside the bedroom where Papa had lain for many weeks, dying of stomach cancer. We were about to have supper, but the tension in the air stopped all thoughts of eating. For a brief moment I got a glance in the bedroom door and saw Mama and my older sister, Emma, feverishly rubbing Papa's legs with alcohol, but then someone closed the door and said, "Y'all go over by the fire, and we will be there in a minute."

Papa was dying. My brother George had just returned from uptown and had bought Papa a chicken salad sandwich from Bolt's Drugstore because Papa loved them so much. Mama had sent my sister, Louise, out to the drugstore to use the telephone to call Dr. Murray. Some men who were there at the drugstore saw Louise's distress and came to our house to see if they could be of help.

Soon we were all sitting around the fire in the dining room, weeping, except for Mama. She had the poker in her hand, and she was chunking the fire and staring her grief into the gray ashes, not shedding a tear. I never saw them take the body out of the house. I never got to say good-bye to Papa.

That night I dreamed everything was all right, only to wake up and be doubly sad. The funeral was on Sunday, but because I had the mumps and stayed home with Azzie, who had come to help out, I did not get to experience that final moment. I was seven years old, and it would be years before I even got to see his gravesite.

He was gone.

But not entirely.

In my early years my body was strong and limber. I could climb a tree monkey-like, especially the big chinaberry tree in our backyard. I knew all the limbs and they knew me. I knew how each would respond to my body as I roamed that tree like a second home. By the time I was ten, it was my place to go be alone, my hiding place, my haven. I loved that tree and it loved me.

One Saturday morning right after breakfast I "flew" to the top of my tree to look out over the village, and then I climbed down to one of the bottom limbs. I was sitting there when I saw a man come from the sidewalk that passed in front of our house toward where I was sitting on my limb. He came to my tree and stood there looking at me for a few long seconds, staring me straight in the eyes. I was not afraid.

He took off his fedora and said, "You need to be careful in that tree—don't fall out and break something."

I had never seen this man before—and yet I knew I him. His smile was gentle, and his hair was split into two hemispheres with a vast ocean of baldness between them.

"What's your name?" he asked softly.

"Billy Hale—what's yours?"

"I'm Bill Hale too."

We looked at each other for a long moment. "Where do you live?" I asked.

"Anywhere I want to live."

There was a certain kind of calmness in the already-gentle stillness of the morning air. "Where are you headed?" I asked.

"Here!" he said and then, "Everything is going to be good, Billy."

With his fedora back on his head, he slowly walked around the side of the house and was *gone.* I never told anyone this story until this pen recorded it just now. Would he come back again?

The Pacific Ocean was so fierce I thought it would destroy and sink the troop ship I was on in May 1945. We were headed to the war zones in the islands of the South Pacific, but that fact did not bother me at the moment. My main concern now was me and the sea. My sleeping hammock swayed constantly, as did all of them, screeching, moaning, and whining. I was four decks below the churning waves of the sea, which meant the ocean was just a few feet outside the steel wall about ten feet from where I tossed in nonsleep. The storm lasted three days, and most of that time I was hung over the toilet, vomiting my soul up, yellow and stinking.

They had warned us of Japanese submarines in the Pacific, and that added to my anxiety, which was off the charts already. The days lost all distinction. One of the sailors told us the captain had said it was the storm of the century. I was scared and sick and could not generate the least moment of valor or bravery.

One night I got up to go up a few decks and look out a porthole that was inside a door leading to the deck. The sea was raging. As I stood there looking into the darkened night, the door opened, and a very wet sailor stepped inside. For a second he stopped, and we both looked out the porthole. He stood close. I could tell he was much older than I was.

"Where are you from, young man?"

"Greenville, South Carolina," I answered. Then I asked, "Where you from?"

"I'm from Greenville too."

"What's your name?"

"I am Bill Hale." He stuck out his hand, and we shook.

"My name is Bill Hale also."

We looked at each other for a penetrating minute.

He tapped me on the shoulder and said, "Billy, things are going to be all right." He opened the door and went out onto the stormy deck, but before he closed the door, he yelled back, "I'll see you again."

As odd as it seems, I noticed he had a fedora in his hand, and then he was *gone*. The storm did finally subside, and I looked for him on the ship for the remainder of the trip to Hawaii, but he had vanished.

One day around noon, while I was tending to my duties as principal, I heard voices in the outer office. My secretary was asking, "Can I tell him who you are?"

A man with a deep voice answered "No, ma'am, I would like to surprise him."

Often my lunch was brought to my desk by the staff of the cafeteria, especially on fried-chicken day. They knew I loved fried gizzards, and on this day they would bring me a big plate of gizzards. I had just finished my gizzards when he walked in.

"So this is how a principal is treated?" the man said, with a big smile.

I came around my desk and we shook hands. He held a gray fedora in his hand. I knew I had seen him someplace, but where?

"I was in town and some folks at the restaurant mentioned your name, and I wanted to come and meet you."

His stomach was prominent, his blue eyes sparkled, and his hair was very thin, with a big bald area in the middle.

"Where are you from, Mister?"

"Oh, I just travel where I need to go."

"Well, what brings you to Gaffney?" I asked.

"Billy, I wanted to see you doing this."

How did he know to call me "Billy"? "And, sir, what's your name?" I asked, but by then I knew. A shaft of sunlight filled the chair where he sat holding his fedora. I knew him but could not speak. We sat, eyes fixed on each other, for how long I did not know.

"Things are all right now, Billy—wouldn't you say?"

Then he was *gone.*

My secretary came in and looked around. "Who were you talking to, Mr. Hale?"

I shuffled and stuttered and said, "I was on the phone."

Would he be back? Perhaps!

There is nothing in the human character more fascinating nor healing than the imagination.

The Wire-Coat-Hanger
Antenna

O NE ASPECT OF MY POSITION at the University of Georgia's
Center for Continuing Education was to attend meetings
in Atlanta, which was seventy miles away. These trips were
mostly over and back the same day. Long before audio tapes and CDs,
my car radio was my constant companion. Also, long before the advent
of talk radio, which now pollutes the airways and our lives, music was
radio's basic feature. Atlantans were blessed with a full-powered, clear-
channel radio station, WSB. In the 1960s, the station's manager was a
true giant in broadcasting. His name was Elmo Ellis, and he was a man
with a deep, resonant voice that was readily recognized throughout the
area by thousands of loyal listeners. Elmo was a voice of progress, along
with Ralph Magill of the *Atlanta Constitution/Journal* and Mayor William
Hartsfield. Elmo Ellis was erudite, aristocratic, and progressive. When he
spoke, you could not help but listen. He was intelligent and intellectual,
clever, cunning, inventive, and involved.

Each broadcast day the station programmed a short three- or four-
minute "thought for the day" from Elmo. They repeated the same one
several times each day. They were pithy, provocative messages, sometimes
humorous, often challenging, and they always made a meaningful point.

Radio reception in those days was not free of static, and there were
periods of weak signals. Good reception depended on the quality of
your antenna, and in our old car that was an issue. My antenna had

been broken in a car wash, and I had put off replacing it. As a makeshift measure, I had the idea that a wire coat hanger bent appropriately might temporarily serve the purpose, and it did. I drove it that way for a while, much to the embarrassment of the family. However, when the family loaded up to go to church, one member of the family would remove it and put it in the floor of the backseat. I would put it back the next day.

On one of my trips to Atlanta, I was driving the old car with the coat-hanger antenna but had to wait until I was very close to Atlanta to tune in WSB so I could hear the best music in town. After a song or two, there he was, Elmo Ellis! I heard him say, "Tennyson once wrote, 'Find a weed and kill it.'"

I was not a devotee of Tennyson, nor had I taken more than a collegiate glance in his direction, but I could not imagine him saying, "Find a weed and kill it."

I carry a folded road map of Georgia on the seat beside me when I drive, and when Elmo said "Find a weed and kill it," I quickly wrote it down on that map, adding the date and Elmo's name. I thought, *Here is something I want to remember.* I listened carefully as Elmo elaborated on the theme with passion and purpose. I was moved by some of the things he said. As he ended the radio spot, he returned to where he had started and said, "Remember, as Mr. Tennyson said, *'Find a need and fill it.'*"

I had received the message but totally missed his point. How often in communicating with others does this happen? I remember laughing out loud when I realized that I had misheard Elmo's statement.

This was such a poignant experience I began including it in my speeches, and audiences liked the story. A few years later I was invited to make an after-dinner speech for the Georgia Association of Broadcasters at their annual meeting on Jekyll Island. I could hardly wait for the opportunity to tell my "real" broadcast story in a speech for broadcasters.

I arrived at the banquet hall of the Holiday Inn on the island and went in to check on the arrangements of the room where I was to speak and to meet the gentleman who had invited me there. "Dr. Hale, I gave your bio information to another person who will introduce you tonight; is that okay?"

"Sure thing!"

At the head table that night, I was seated next to a very charming lady who told me that her husband, who was to introduce me, had been delayed by a telephone call but would be there shortly. The evening opened with a prayer by a broadcaster who had obviously been called into broadcasting from the pulpit because he waxed and mumbled, long past patience, before he said, "Amen!"

After the prayer I saw a very tall, distinctive man enter the room and come toward the head table. The lady seated next to me stood up and said, "Dr. Hale, I would like for you to meet my husband, Elmo Ellis." I stood to shake his hand and looked up into his broad smile.

"Mr. Hale, I have been asked to introduce you this evening."

I was stunned and delighted at the honor of being introduced by one of the nation's broadcast icons. Elmo used the standard material I had sent but ended his remarks, "Here is Bill Hale, a young man making his mark on public broadcasting in this country."

Did he really say that about me?

I made my presentation including my find-a-weed-and-kill-it story, saying to them, "I hope you get either my message or my point tonight, but if you missed both, then we really have a problem." When I finished there was a standing ovation, but I still think it was for Elmo, not for me!

Afterward Elmo thanked me for coming and said, "May I use that story on the air someday?"

I never heard it on air, but that did not matter, because the big man had made me feel like a giant. And it had all started with me trying to listen to my car radio using a wire coat hanger for an antenna.

There are many antics that my family tell about me these days as we gather for Sunday lunches or for special birthday parties, but none get the traction any more than the story of the wire coat hanger I used as an antenna on my car.

Me and the Beyond

THROUGHOUT THESE PAGES I HAVE made many references to the church and my life in it. My theology has been an evolving one, always moving toward a more rational view, a position where I find great comfort and meaning. Therefore, I think it is incumbent on me to finish this book with the following thoughts.

Each morning before the sun rises, I walk about one hundred feet to retrieve the morning paper and yesterday's mail, thinking, *Good morning, Mister God! Happy day to you*, or *Good morning, Brother, Sister, Mother, Uncle, Friend, God*. I do this because my meditation needs vary from day to day, and I desire a particular type of "other presence." All along the driveway I scatter my major concerns for the day. This is not an attempt to pray. It is merely a connection with the "beyond."

The beyond in my life has taken on as many shapes as snowflakes, as many colors as an assorted jar of jelly beans, or as many varieties as Heinz has pickles. The beyond in my life has been like an ever-present shadow, a constant source of presence and consideration from my first days of self-awareness. There was always me and my other—the shadow—and we have evolved together over the decades.

In my early days, God was a man, sort of an old man, who lived in heaven and directed things like storms and stuff. He kept score on everybody in order to decide who would come to heaven and who would go to hell. Not unlike Santa Claus, he knew everything you did, good and bad, and if you were bad you got a lump of coal in your stocking, and if you were good you got a toy. The word "god" was used a lot around the church but not much around our house, except when Papa fell down the back step ("Them goddamn steps gonna kill me yet!").

The word "god" was not capitalized in my mind in those early days. Somewhere, perhaps in a book at school, I had seen a picture of god. It was probably the classic scene from the Sistine Chapel in the Vatican. After that I knew what god looked like. He had on a long white gown. He had a long beard and was not smiling. The man his finger was touching was butt naked.

Time passed and the not-smiling god turned into a "mean" sort of man-thing who would do something bad to you if you "did a sin." This idea stayed around a long time, and I was constantly dealing with the watchful eye of god, which lurked around the corners everywhere I went, especially at church and at the movies.

At the age of eleven or twelve I got "saved" at a revival meeting, and things began to change because I was now on "god's side" The god became a fixed set of thoughts centered around Jesus, the Bible, and church attendance. Do good, be kind, help others, go to church, give the tithe, be clean, and abide by a huge avalanche of "don'ts." God faded into the background, and his son took center stage. I was taught that the Baptists had it all right. Other churches were wrong, including the Methodists and Presbyterians. Jews, Catholics, and other "pagans/heathens" were not going to heaven but instead to the furnace of hell, which was provided especially for them. These ridiculous concepts were what I took to the army with me at the age of eighteen.

When it was my turn for the smiling captain at the induction center to interview me as a new inductee into the army, he motioned for me to sit down at the table. The first question he asked was, "Son, are you a Protestant, Catholic, or Jew?" "I am a Baptist, sir." I did not say this with any particular pride, just a matter of fact. I said it because I had never heard the word *Protestant*. However, I knew I was not Catholic or Jewish. It was at that moment that I found out I was a Protestant, but it would be many years before I understood what that meant.

Two years of military life during WWII were a time of amazing reassessment of things religious for me. The beyond lost most of its personal applications for me. Others around me worshipped their gods, and even though they were not like mine, it was the same idea. God was something way out in space who watched over us, Protestants, Catholics and Jews. My restrictive and traditional concepts of God were coming out of the closet. How could I live with those fascinating, interesting men and not respect their beliefs or observe how they lived their lives? They were so free from the "Hound of Heaven" that was constantly breathing down my collar. I compared my life to the lives I saw them living. There was Lazarus, a tall New York Jewish boy, who was funny and happy; he became my friend. He commented, "Reb, you sure do talk funny." He really was not a pagan, as I had been taught. Most of the boys in my training company were Catholic. They were just regular guys like me. They had their crosses and went to Mass each week. Slowly, imperceptibly, I was changing. My village god began to disappear, to be replaced with new ideas.

In my basic training at Camp Blanding, Florida, our battalion chaplain was a kind-faced Presbyterian whose sermons were more like chats, totally unlike the red-faced tirades at my church back home. He said, "The good God will take care of you and be at your side to call on no matter what happens." What a different idea! God was not hovering over me like an invisible cloud but was a source I could to turn to if need be. Actually, I had never wanted God to be close around me. At this point in the evolution of my faith, the word *God* became capitalized in my mind. God switched from a dreaded future judge to a new presence. The image of God softened, but He was still in a place called heaven, somewhere "up there," which I accepted as if it were pure, unquestionable science.

Upon my release from the army in 1946, the astoundingly generous GI Bill of Rights gave me the life-changing opportunity to enroll at Furman University. While I was there, I majored in education and minored in religion. Somewhere in one of those religion classes, I heard the idea that God was spirit, not some physical wizard in the sky who knew all things, could do all things, and directed all things. This walloping idea took years of processing, but I plowed great theological soil trying to cultivate this newness. I knew a domino had fallen, but I did not know the consequences at the time. Dominoes do have a way of knocking over other dominoes.

I married Helen, my high-school sweetheart, in 1946, and we knew we had family and cultural traditions to uphold. We were both from mill village–style churches where the expectation was to conform rather than question what was said and preached. Going to church became one of the driving ingredients in our family.

After finishing college, I became a teacher of world history in the high school in Gaffney, South Carolina. Gaffney was a conservative community, steeped in traditions. The students I was teaching were the same age group I taught in the First Baptist Church Sunday school. However, I was living in a personal intellectual battleground. I had not yet become a reader, and I was in over my head trying to learn enough history to teach it. I had little desire to expand my personal theological horizons, even though I doubted greatly the idea of the "young earth" mentality. I dismissed the creation story by telling them that however God wanted to do it was fine with me and that I believed the biblical seven days did not necessarily mean seven days as we knew them. Wow! I had said more than I knew and far less than I knew at the same time.

During this time of my life I was an evangelical young man who believed it was essential that these boys and girls get "saved." When I became the principal of that same high school, on an occasion I would pull off an "evangelical stunt" with some students who had gotten in trouble at school. God was highly operational and significant in my life and work. I still tried to avoid creating any mental imagery of God as spirit.

The next phase of my life was graduate school at Florida State University. This should have been the place where I made some major adjustments in my theology, because I was thrust into many new situations where differences among people were pronounced. But at that time I was stiff-backed and set in my ways. A Mr. Tadros was a doctoral student in my department, a sweet, gentle man from Egypt, and a Coptic Christian.

In a philosophy class one day, he spoke of his faith, and I was impressed with his knowledge and passion. Being with him and accepting him caused my mental space to open a bit—but not much. I still had it in my mind that God was somewhere out there and wanted all human beings to come to heaven, but if you chose to reject God's desire you would be sent to hell forever.

While in graduate study, I began to read an occasional article or book in the big world of the sciences. Cosmology intrigued me most of all. It was there I began to sense the vastness of "it." I also was stunned by what I learned to call *deep time*—the vast age of the universes. My theological bucket was beginning to leak!

Settling at the University of Georgia in Athens, in 1961, placed me in constant contact with the intellectual community, and over the course of time most of my faith-factor beliefs came under close examination. The next forty years of my life as a Bible teacher were a slow process of becoming a skeptic. I was a good teacher and kept at it with verve and vigor, but I waged an inner battle with the Baptist ideas. I especially questioned the practice of missionaries being sent to people who had a viable faith. It was an insult, but the Baptists were convinced that all human beings must come to God through the "power" of Jesus, no exceptions!

I began to seek enlightened preachers and other campus thinkers who dared to interpret the Bible as great literature, and to punctuate my world with doubts about the book's infallibility. My predictable, absolute God began to come apart. I had been warned that a logical mind was the devil's playground and once reason came to live with you, you could never go back to the old comfortable cocoon of your past—and this warning was valid. When the belief system of Christianity, as well as the beliefs of the Abrahamic tradition in general, started to fall into disarray, it was like a mile-long stack of dominoes waiting for the first one to fall. And fall they did!

Ideas such as the *second coming* and *eternity* were absurd, and I knew it. *Salvation* and *sin* made no more sense than Santa coming down the chimney. I discovered that the human quest and urge to live on and on was the genesis of the whole fabric of religions. Millions of probing minds, over tens of thousands of years, imagined and created systems of thought that made eternal life "possible." I taught myself to accept the finality of biological life as being all there is, except that my human spirit will be around as long as any one remembers me. This is not fatalism! It is the freedom to live life to the fullest extent possible without the smoke and mirrors about some future *beyond*. However, I maintained all the accoutrements and social aspects of the Christian way. I went to church and served a leadership role, taught Sunday school, and felt successful there. I did this while privately enjoying the real world of my imagination.

It took me a long time, but I finally accepted the Bible as history without any historical facts. It is a grand book written to tell the Hebrew idea of God. Their creation story is as good as any of the other mythic creation stories of antiquity, and all of them are products of the creative imagination of the human mind.

Mythology, biology, paleontology, astronomy, anthropology, archeology, cosmology, physics, religious art, and geology slowly trumped theology as the places to find meaningful knowledge and a place to stand. I was particularly turned off by the long history of the world's religions, including Christianity, battling against the rise of intellect and reason. I had been an unwitting advocate of this anti-intellectualism by continuing to teach the content of the biblical story.

After years of reading, attending university lectures, and meeting several notable theologians for conversation, I came to realize that the concepts of sin and salvation were absurdities foisted on the human scene in order to control human behavior. Human beings had simply evolved over the past two hundred thousand years as *Homo sapiens*, the "thinking being," and there is nothing wrong with us except those things that evolution and our DNA cause us to be.

The church taught me that I was depraved from birth based on the cockeyed thinking of Augustine in the fifth century. His coinage of the idea of *original sin* is a despicable bit of nonsense that came into the dogma early in the Christian movement. It is an astoundingly divisive factor among the human race and is based on the mythic story of the creation of male and female in the folklore of the Hebrew people.

Here, in the winter of my time as a part of the saga of life, I have come to the end of my belief in the commonly held origins of all the world's religions. I did this on my own mental playground, prompted by my imagination. All—let me emphasize—*all* of the structure of all world religions is a product of the magnificent, monumental, marvelous, accumulative imagination of the human being. We, the human race, invented, created, cultivated, and codified, this imagined world into many great religions, which have served civilizations in varied ways throughout the course of human history. These "gods" of the human imagination I can revere and even worship, meaning I can stand in awe of their development. I do not need nor do I believe there is an entity that is the "beyond." I can and do transpose the imagined God into the literature, music, and prayers of the Christian church with relative ease and great comfort. Attending church has become for me a much-desired activity because of the quietness, the beauty of the literature, the power of the music, and the presence of people who are seeking comfort in the human spirit. Churches and all places of worship are the meetinghouses where people with different worldviews come together and harmonize their spirits around grand old traditions.

For more years than I know I have lived in the unexpressed but strongly felt world of the human spirit. I think the most unquenchable fire in the world is the human spirit. In my world of thought, the so-called work of the Holy Spirit is really the human spirit functioning at peak energy and insight. Unlike breath, which we all seem to have a fairly equal capacity for, the human spirit is a developmental feature. We make our own choices. The experiences we have help our human spirits to grow and glow. In every generation, in every cluster of humans, there are a few who advance and enhance the human spirit from the ordinary to the extraordinary level: Jesus, Mohammed, Michelangelo, Jefferson, Mother Teresa, Gandhi, and King. They all had abundance of human spirit, and they expressed it in myriad fashions.

My purpose for living has been to dwell in the human community, to help others to enhance their spirits, to light my candle, and to assist others to keep their spirit glowing. In the end, I wish to feel that I have added to the great, rich, accumulative human imagination some small measure of energy, which perhaps will enhance and promote the collective incomprehensible human spirit. For what else do we live?

About the Author

FOR MORE THAN A HALF century the author was a nationally sought-after professional speaker and seminar leader in the emerging field of human awareness. An area of study distinct from human relations, its aim is to keep in the forefront of leadership and executive development the human side of the environment. Bill Hale has degrees from Furman University and the University of South Carolina, and a doctorate in foundations of education from Florida State University. The driving element in his presentations was always his stories of family and friends. These stories were used to underscore the content of the speeches and seminars.

Bill Hale has lived into his ninth decade, during which time he was a drum major of an army band, teacher, school administrator, professor, director of a continuing education center, television executive and producer, writer, husband, father, grandfather, and great-grandfather. He is an avid reader, devotee of musical theater, community volunteer, and activist, as well as a humanist with deep roots in Christian traditions.

Acclaimed by many as a philosopher, provocateur, and a darned good cook, he lives in Athens, Georgia, with his wife, Helen, and all their children live nearby. As he whimsically says, "We are not rich, but we are significant."